COURAGEOUS LIVING

Courageous Living

Charles Simpson

with
Dave and Neta Jackson

VINE
BOOKS

Servant Publications
Ann Arbor, Michigan

Vine Books is an imprint of Servant Publications especially
designed to serve Evangelical Christians.

Scripture quotations are from the New American Standard
Bible, © The Lockman Foundation 1960, 1962, 1963, 1968,
1971, 1972, 1973, 1975, 1977.

Cover design by Charles Piccirilli
Cover photo by Tom Grill/Comstock, Inc.

Published by Servant Books
P.O. Box 8617
Ann Arbor, Michigan 48107

Printed in the United States of America
ISBN 0-89283-334-3
87 88 89 90 10 9 8 7 6 5 4 3 2 1

Contents

We should by all means
go up and take possession of it,
for we shall surely overcome it.
(Numbers 13:30)

Preface

FOR THE LAST FIFTY YEARS or so we have been conditioned by our society to be very introspective. Many of us have benefited from some of that, but it is easy to get so lost in trying to understand ourselves that we fail to understand what God is saying to us. God has a reason for our living that is beyond ourselves—beyond self-fulfillment, beyond self-awareness, beyond introspection.

I like to study the lives of people who lived for something beyond themselves and found happiness and meaning in that. The Bible has taught me that true fulfillment came to people of action who gave their lives for something that was greater than themselves.

This is a season to act. Both in the church and in the nation there is a mood change among Christians. This is becoming a time of action. We are becoming restless with analysis that doesn't lead anywhere.

Hebrews 11 tells us why God favored such people as Abraham and Moses, Sarah and Rahab, and many others. They were acclaimed because they "by faith conquered kingdoms, performed acts of righteousness, obtained promises, shut the mouths of lions, quenched the power of fire, escaped the edge of the sword, from weakness were made strong, became mighty in war, put foreign armies to flight" (33, 34). These were people of action. Daniel 11:32 says, "... the people who know their God will display strength and take action." We want to be an active rather than a passive people.

One of the most dramatic stories of action in the Bible is the conquest of the Promised Land by the Israelites. And so, in this book, I want to study the beginning of that story (the conquest of Jericho) with you in such a way that we, too, can be challenged to take the land, challenged as a church to move forward in holy action to take from the enemy what belongs to God, and challenged to defeat the enemy's strongholds in our own lives.

This is a story of war as real and relevant as the evening news, but we are given God's behind-the-scenes commentary on the transcendent scope, unique weapons, and necessary strategy for victory.

ONE

The Cause for War

W E DIDN'T START THIS WAR. We were born into it. Some may be so numb to it that they ask, "What war?" This war is every evil, every crime, all deceitfulness, all suffering, and every human battle that has ever been fought—whether with angry voices, courtroom tricks, swords and spears, guns and tanks, or bombs and missiles. These are earthly manifestations of a cosmic war that has been going on since Satan's rebellion.

The origins of this war are described in Revelation 12:7-9:

> And there was war in heaven, Michael and his angels waging war with the dragon. And the dragon and his angels waged war, and they were not strong enough, and there was no longer a place found for them in heaven. And the great dragon was thrown down, the serpent of old who is called the devil and Satan, who deceives the whole world; he was thrown down to the earth, and his angels were thrown down with him.

Satan, our enemy from before the beginning of time, wanted to be as God, and he sowed subterfuge and deception, discord and subversion. That's how the enemy works; he militates against the truth. In fact, his efforts at deceit have convinced many people that there is no war. But "The Lord is a warrior" (Ex 15:3) and he leads us into battle. God turns the light of truth on the devil and his ways. Light allows you to see what is really there. Our Lord defeats the devil with truth. Scripture says, "You shall know the truth, and the truth shall make you free" (Jn 8:32).

In Psalm 45:3-6 we read:

Gird Thy sword on Thy thigh, O Mighty One, In Thy splendor and Thy majesty! / And in Thy majesty ride on victoriously, / For the cause of truth and meekness and righteousness; / Let Thy right hand teach Thee awesome things. / Thine arrows are sharp; / The peoples fall under Thee; / Thine arrows are in the heart of the King's enemies. /Thy throne, O God, is forever and ever.

In effect, the writer says, "Lord, gird on your sword for the cause of truth. Don't let truth falter for lack of your power. Do awesome things, Lord; do fearful things; do frightening things. Then the Lord's arrows will be in the heart of his enemies."

A major objective in this war is to advance truth. You don't get truth by accident; somebody has to fight for it. Truth is not a thing that comes to you just because you were born. There are places in this world where you couldn't find out the truth even if you were willing to buy it, and there are places in this world where you'd be in trouble if you spoke the truth. Truth is a cause that someone has to fight for if it's to be obtained and maintained.

No, we didn't start this war. The war was already going on, and we were born into the middle of it. But ultimately, in your life, you have to choose which side you're going to be on. You have to choose either to say, "There is such a thing as truth," or "I don't know, and I don't care," in which case you really stand with deception. But we're all forced into the choice; we can't be neutral.

The Scripture says the enemy's weapon against people is

deception; he is the deceiver. He fights against the truth. That's why truth is that which can never be taken for granted. But not only is it something we must *fight for*, it is also what we *fight with*. God's weapon is truth. Revelation 19:15 says that Jesus is coming with a sharp sword going out of his mouth. That means his words of truth destroy the words of deception that the enemy spreads around. The real war is between truth and lies.

This war, which began in heaven, now encompasses the earth. But Scripture, with its timeless perspective, tells us the outcome. It says, in Revelation 12:11, that the brethren—all of us who believe—overcame the enemy by means of three factors: "the blood of the Lamb," that is, Christ's sacrificial death; "the word" of our "testimony," which is, in fact, the truth, the Word of God; and no love for this life—we must be willing to fight, "even to death."

Loving this life will let the enemy defeat us. We can't really win any war while trying to preserve our own lives at the same time. Our confidence in God must enable us to lay down our lives in whatever way is required of us in order to win the war.

The Scope of the War

We must be careful to understand that this war is transcendent, not temporal.

1. Our enemy is not people. Ephesians 6:12 tells us, "For we wrestle not against flesh and blood" (KJV). The verse continues to tell us what we *are* against. We are "against principalities, against powers, against the rulers of the darkness of this world, against spiritual wickedness in high places." It is a much more serious realm than mere flesh and blood in which we must do battle. The outcome of things in the natural world is determined in the spiritual realm.

2. Guns and tanks are not our weapons. "For though we walk in the flesh, we do not war according to the flesh, for the weapons of our warfare are not of the flesh, but divinely powerful for the destruction of fortresses" (2 Cor 10:3, 4). Our ultimate weapons are spiritual because we're ultimately dealing with spiritual things. In fact, depending upon mere physical weapons while ignoring the battlefield on which the real victory will be determined would deceive us with a false sense of security.

Four Presuppositions

There are also four presuppositions about this war that I'd like to offer.

1. The gospel is a battle cry. Spiritual war is inherent in the Great Commission. Jesus said, "Go therefore and make disciples of all the nations, baptizing them in the name of the Father and the Son and the Holy Spirit, teaching them to observe all that I commanded you" (Mt 28:19, 20a). The Great Commission presupposes a spiritual war because Satan doesn't want the truth disseminated; he does not want the gospel to be spread. And not everyone wants to be a disciple. The Muslim world, for instance, wants no part of the gospel of Jesus Christ. The Marxist world wants no part of the gospel of Jesus Christ. Jesus didn't say, "Go and disciple all those *except* those that don't want it." He said to go to all the nations, and that will automatically elicit opposition.

2. You must know why you fight. Spiritual war requires an understanding of *why* the battle must be fought and won. It requires a discipline of your will—any kind of war does. You shouldn't go to war if you don't know why you're fighting. The United States has had two recent examples of this lesson. The Korean War was called a "police action," and the Vietnam War was an undeclared war. Many people were involved who had no idea why they were fighting. In fact, in the case of Vietnam, our nation as a whole didn't know or didn't agree on why it was fighting. It is foolish for a nation to fight a war when the reasons are unclear or disputed. The lack of understanding erodes the will to fight. The philosophical underpinings and commitment are missing.

The same is true for the Christian. If you're going to fight a war, you need to know why you're fighting it. If you're going to lay down your life, you need to know why you're doing it.

3. Distractions and passivity lead to defeat. Distractions and passivity will have bad consequences. If you become distracted from the war that is raging between right and wrong, good and evil, the consequences will continue nevertheless. The fighting doesn't stop and wait until you get your mind back on the struggle. Likewise, if, in the face of evil, you become passive, the consequences will run right over you. They will crush you. There is no mercy from the evil one.

4. The spiritual and physical are related. There is a relationship between the spiritual and the physical. You can't yield to spiritual evil and not pay physical consequences. It does matter what spiritual forces are influencing the world. Remember, Satan's goal is destruction and his main weapon is deceit—that is, spreading lies and false ideas.

Some people want you to believe that ideas are harmless. But it mattered when Nazism spread through Europe. There were consequences. And hasn't Marxism mattered to millions who have lost their lives under it or who have been oppressed by it? Hasn't the spread of the Kingdom of God been severely hindered by it, by "just an idea," a lie breaking in from the spiritual realm? It really does matter who runs the world. It really does matter if we turn the world over to secular humanism. It matters because there is a relationship between philosophy and physical events, between theology and physical events.

From the time of Nebuchadnezzar, 600 B.C., until World War II, the Jews were often persecuted and even slaughtered. Although some prospered, the race as a whole was relegated to ghettos, and the collective will of the race was often broken. Only the purpose and power of God could have sustained their ability to pass on their culture in the face of such persecution. The movie, *Fiddler on the Roof,* depicts the poverty and persecution that existed near the end of the last century and at the end of the reign of the Czars in Russia.

Hitler expanded this persecution in the Holocaust, slaughtering six million Jews. While Hitler carried out his extermination, European governments and churches were virtually silent. But what's even more tragic is that sometimes the Jews themselves were silent in the face of their own systematic destruction. Neville Chamberlain, the prime minister of England, became the symbol of the policy of appeasement and passivity. Finally, as Hitler devoured Eastern Europe and moved into Western Europe, the world began to awaken to the reality of his threats.

Europe began to realize that evil exists, and it doesn't go away by ignoring it or appeasing it. Millions of lives lost and long years of horror and pain were part of the great price paid to learn a very bitter lesson.

But was the lesson learned? The Jews learned it. They came away from that experience with a new slogan: "Never again!" What about Europe? What about the United States? If history tells us anything, it tells us that people forget history. Moral confusion—thinking that evil ideas don't matter—led Europe to be silent in the face of this century's greatest terrorists, and moral confusion continues to paralyze Western nations in the face of terrorist intimidation.

Lies That Deny the Cause for War

What are some of the lies that Satan spreads to make people think there is no cause for war? I want to name seven:

Lie #1: There is no right and wrong. Often philosophy, and even theology, does not acknowledge the existence of right and wrong. Many young people have grown up without a sense of right and wrong. Many who were told one thing was right and another thing was wrong, were never adequately told why.

Therefore, they do not have a moral conscience, a moral substructure, to continue to support that judgment in time of doubt or questioning.

We unwittingly help Satan spread this lie when we make rash and dogmatic judgments about right and wrong even though we do not have a sound basis to do so. Then, when our simplistic claims fall apart (under examination), our whole perspective suffers. It would be better to be bold where there is certainty and cautious when we don't know.

We make another error when we presume that right and wrong are necessarily embodied in opposing temporal forces. There have been times when some human institutions, governments, and individuals have rather fully represented truth, liberty, justice—even righteousness. But more often motives are mixed, and sometimes it is hard to imagine that either side is more right than the other. There is a genuine right and wrong, and we need to be well informed and suspicious of the quick and easy answer if we are to fight successfully for the truth.

Lie #2: There is no purpose beyond self-preservation. While studying human behavior, psychologist Abraham Maslow developed his "pyramid of hierarchical needs," which suggests that unless a person's basic needs for self-preservation are met, the person will not be able to function in more noble ways.

His observations were probably quite accurate in terms of the selfish way most humans behave—a true reading of human depravity. But not everyone operates that way, and we do too little to publicize the model men and women who have laid down their lives in living sacrifice or even in death for others. But that is the gospel message. Christ is our chief example. There is an eternal existence beyond this life, and there are values which, because they are eternal, are more precious than life itself.

Lie #3: It's not your fight. Today we seem to lack a sense of responsibility to defend the family, freedom, and rights of others. We condemn those who stand by while a group of men gang rape a woman on a pool table, and yet we are not very worried when religious freedoms are violated, just because it's in another town or state or country. It is a lie of Satan to tell us it's not our fight. Tragically, when we are under attack, there may be no one to come to our aid.

Lie #4: Freedom is not that important. A loss of relationship to our religious and national heritage and a loss of appreciation for its distinctive values has diluted our willingness to fight. Many young people and adults have lost contact with history. They have no real understanding why an early Christian leader like Polycarp would accept martyrdom rather than choose life as a fugitive, or how a statesman like Patrick Henry could have ever said such a thing as, "Give me liberty, or give me death." They have no comprehension of the dynamics that moved them to such dramatic actions.

Lie #5: All men are basically good. Naiveté about human depravity and its potential for gross evil is a lie that tempts us not to fight in hopes that the enemy will settle down if just given a little time and understanding. If you do not believe in right and wrong, the chances are you do not believe in human depravity, and you will underestimate men like Adolf Hitler, Joseph Stalin, or Moammar Gadhafi.

Lie #6: Death is the end, so never risk it. Without an eternal perspective, people think the only life they have is this one, so they will not be willing to risk losing it. The Bible, of course, teaches us that physical death is not the end of life. Ignorance of Scripture and of Christian history leaves one without models to follow. The Book of Hebrews, *Fox's Book of Christian Martyrs, Martyrs' Mirror,* and stories of modern martyrs give us a healthy and inspiring review of men and women willing to lay down their lives for truth.

Lie #7: Compromise is the civilized way to settle differences. Compromise may indeed be a way to settle some differences, but compromise with evil is appeasement. Secular humanism in our society spreads this lie to new generations without regard to what's happened in the past. We seem to take no lessons from the humiliation of the mainstream churches in Europe in the 1930s and 1940s, and we take no inspiration from those in the confessing church who risked all to oppose Hitler and Nazism. As a result, much of our political, educational, and religious communities continue to produce the same kind of citizens that gave us World War II.

To uphold the light of God's truth against these lies is the reason we should enter the war. We have the reason, but are we willing to fight?

TWO

The Will to War

I T IS NOT MY PURPOSE TO INSTILL in us a desire for war, certainly not spiritual war, which, though we sometimes don't realize it, is worse than physical combat. War is a terrible thing. Rather, it's my intention to reestablish a philosophical base for upholding the truth whatever it costs us.

Let's look at the Hebrew nation in the Old Testament, and see how their warfare relates to us. What can we learn? Exodus 13:17 says:

> Now it came about when Pharaoh had let the people go, that God did not lead them by the way of the land of the Philistines, even though it was near; for God said, "Lest the people change their minds when they see war, and they return to Egypt."

Did you ever look at a map and wonder why the Israelites didn't take the shortcut from Egypt up to Canaan? It was just a few days' journey. All they had to do was follow the route around the Mediterranean and they'd have been there. But the Scripture says that God didn't lead them that way because they would have run right into the fortified Philistine cities, and the Philistines were men of war.

The Bible gives us the reason why God didn't lead them straight in to the Promised Land. God knew that if they encountered the Philistines and subsequent war, they would have turned around and gone the other way. They would have preferred slavery to war.

That's our choice, too—slavery or war. The Israelites would have preferred to go back and live under the Egyptian yoke rather than face the prospect of being killed. That's a serious choice. People who fail to deal forthrightly with issues may seem to be making some fairly rational decisions, and they may actually be making the "safer" decision—at least for a time. But they are only delaying the inevitable.

God says that he couldn't bring them into the land because they couldn't face the issue of war. So, he had to lead them the long way around, which included a trek into the wilderness for a period of time. Scripture doesn't say that God didn't lead them into the land because he would not have been able to defeat the Philistines, but because the Israelites would have turned back. If you turn back, God can't fight for you. If you are afraid to meet issues, you'll never know the power of God. We're not just talking about a fear of swords and spears or tanks and jets. We're talking about the ability to face the enemy under any circumstances. The principle is the same whether it is on a physical battlefield or in our spiritual lives.

But what do we need to be able to face war?

We Cannot Have a Slave Mentality

When the Israelites came out of Egypt they had a low self-image. Their wills had been broken in Egypt, so God gave them a few months of rehabilitation. But even though great miracles occurred in the wilderness and they were following a great leader like Moses, they remained essentially only slaves that had been set free.

It is easier to get the slave out of physical bondage than to get the slave mentality out of the people. It is one thing to have your freedom declared to you, but it is another to change your image of yourself. The consequences of enslavement are far beyond the servitude itself. It takes years to get over thinking like a slave. Every Christian faces this because at one time you were enslaved to sin, and it takes a period of time to realize that you are not only free, you are more powerful than the sin. It's easier for God to get you out of sin than it is for you to change your mind about your power over sin.

The Israelites would have backed away from war because they were still slaves in their minds. They were slaves to fear. When the spirit and will are broken by slavery, it takes time to restore them. May God help us never to be enslaved in our minds and in our spirits.

We Must Foster Courage

We continue the account of the Israelites after they've experienced months of God's dealing with them in the wilderness. Finally, they come to Kadesh where they send out spies to evaluate Canaan. Numbers 13:23-33 says:

> "Then they came to the valley of Eshcol and from there cut down a branch with a single cluster of grapes; and they carried it on a pole between two men, with some of the pomegranates and the figs. [This was quite a bunch of grapes; it took two men to carry it on a pole.] That place was called the valley of Eshcol, because of the cluster which the sons of Israel cut down from there.
>
> When they returned from spying out the land, at the end of forty days, they proceeded to come to Moses and Aaron and to all the congregation of the sons of Israel in the wilderness of Paran, at Kadesh; and they brought back word to them and to all the congregation and showed them the fruit of the land. Thus they told him, and said, "We went in to the land where you sent us; and it certainly does flow with milk and honey, and this is its fruit. Nevertheless, the people

who live in the land are strong, and the cities are fortified and very large; and moreover, we saw the descendants of Anak there. Amalek is living in the land of the Negev and the Hittites and the Jebusites and the Amorites are living in the hill country, and the Canaanites are living by the sea and by the side of the Jordan."

Then Caleb quieted the people before Moses, and said, "We should by all means go up and take possession of it, for we shall surely overcome it." But the men who had gone up with him said, "We are not able to go up against the people, for they are too strong for us." [You can see their low self-image, their lack of confidence, and their lack of faith in God.] So they gave out to the sons of Israel a bad report of the land which they had spied out, saying, "The land through which we have gone, in spying it out, is a land that devours its inhabitants; and all the people whom we saw in it are men of great size. There also we saw the Nephilim (the sons of Anak are part of the Nephilim) [In Jewish tradition the angels intermarried with the daughters of men and produced great giants of supernatural origin. Not only are we dealing with Hittites and Canaanites, but now we are dealing with the Nephilim]; and we became like grass-hoppers in our own sight, and so we were in their sight."

Did you know that your enemy will see you the same way you see yourself? You won't fool the devil. He knows what you really think about what God will do on your behalf.

We Must Be Confident of the Reward

The Israelites said their enemies were too strong for them, so they made a decision to retreat. They took a natural view of things, a negative view of things, and they drew back. They decided they weren't going to go into the land. They threw away their confidence. Hebrews 10:35 says, "Do not throw away your confidence," because after you've suffered for a while, it will bring "a great reward." Now the writer didn't say, "Don't throw away your theology." That's not what most people throw away on a daily basis. He said, "Do not throw away your confidence." Then he quoted the Lord in verse 38: "If any man draw back, my soul shall have no pleasure in him" (KJV).

God doesn't appreciate "drawbacks." There are halfbacks and fullbacks, and there are "drawbacks." It seems that on every team you have a few. There's always someone who says, "Wow, Nephilim. Now we need to think about this. Let's not be hasty. Let's not rush into this; let's meditate on it a while longer," while the enemy continues to run over us.

The Israelites made a decision to retreat. They came to the edge, saw the giants, and drew back.

We Must Know the Consequences of Cowardice

Numbers 33 is a story about the Israelites' long journey to nowhere. It's one of those chapters like the genealogies—when you get to it in your devotions, you just turn two pages.

Once the Israelites made a decision to retreat, they began a long, unnecessary journey to nowhere. If you read the names of the places they traveled through, you may think they went somewhere, but most were just watering holes. Many didn't even have a name; the Israelites had to name them when they got there. If you check the translations, some of them mean things like *wild place* and *depression and humility* and *heap of ruins* and *terror* and *wandering*. None of the names means *the Lord is bountiful* or *the Lord is faithful* or *the Lord is abundant* or *blessed are those that believe*. No. They mean *welcome to misery for forty years*.

These people decided not to enter the land because they were afraid to die. But notice what happened: they died anyway! We are going to die anyway, too. The issue is not whether or not we are going to die, but what are we going to die *for*? They died for nothing.

When the Israelites first came up to the Promised Land, they had been primed by God. They had been delivered by the power of God and had come through a sea that he had dried up. They came to this land by the power of God. But when they looked the situation in the face, they began to perspire and they drew back.

In Numbers 14 we read that they turned around with a vengeance. And isn't that just the way it is? When you encounter a challenge as you follow the will of God and you turn back, you don't usually turn back casually. You turn back angry and bitter and a candidate for spiritual infection. There's self-justification and complaint, and the enemy rushes in. From then on there's death.

That's exactly what happened to these people. Look at Numbers 14:1-5:

> Then all the congregation lifted up their voices and cried, and the people wept that night. [When the spies came back and said it was a good land but the enemy was too mighty, there wasn't shouting and praising God. No, there was misery.] And all the sons of Israel grumbled against Moses and Aaron [That's what they had been doing for three months; they talked themselves out of the land.]; and the whole congregation said to them, "Would that we had died in the land of Egypt! Or would that we had died in this wilderness! [Do you see what they asked for? They got their wish.] And why is the Lord bringing us into this land, to fall by the sword? Our wives and our little ones will become plunder; would it not be better for us to return to Egypt?" So they said to one another, "Let us appoint a leader and return to Egypt." [So they resorted to the democratic process to find a leader who would do what they wanted him to do.] Then Moses and Aaron fell on their faces in the presence of all the assembly of the congregation of the sons of Israel.

Moses and Aaron, with the help of Joshua and Caleb, begged the people not to go back. But it was too late.

We Must Understand God's Compelling Purposes

In verse 20, the Lord says, "I have pardoned them according to your word" (Nm 14:20). As a result of Moses' appeal on behalf of the people, God forgave them, but he wouldn't let them go into the land.

> ". . . but indeed, as I live, all the earth will be filled with the glory of the Lord. Surely all the men who have seen My glory and My signs, which I performed in Egypt and in the wilderness, yet have put Me to the test these ten times and have not listened to My voice, shall by no means see the land which I swore to their fathers, nor shall any of those who spurned Me see it. But My servant Caleb, because he has had a different spirit and has followed Me fully, I will bring into the land which he entered, and his descendants shall take possession of it." (Nm 14:21-24)

Consider verse 21 again: "Indeed, as I live, all the earth will be filled with the glory of the Lord." When the Lord says, "*as I live*," whatever he says next is never going to change. It's permanent.

"As I live, all the earth will be filled with the glory of the Lord." This is God's abiding purpose. God doesn't draw back when people draw back. This statement was not made in a revival meeting when emotion is on "high." It wasn't made in the Book of Acts when things were going well. It wasn't made when the people of God had done some great thing, and the Lord was inspired to say, "As I live, all the earth will be filled with the glory of the Lord." No. This is God's statement in the darkest hour when the people were retreating and running. God said in effect, "You can go back if you want to. But let me tell you something; a generation is coming that won't go back. As I live, all the earth—not just this land—all the earth will be filled with the glory of the Lord."

As surely as there is a God, the purpose of God won't go away. And that's a compelling reason for us to fight.

We Need a New Spirit

You may not have the will to go to war, you may not be able to face the issues, you may not want to deal with them, but God will deal with them, with or without you. He's going to find a people who will deal with them. In Israel's case, there was a generation coming that would enter the land.

Caleb had to wait forty years for this to come to pass. But God said, "I like his spirit." Caleb had said, "We can take the land. We can do it." God said in effect, "I like him. I'll let him last those forty years. I'll let him survive those thousands of funerals—scores of funerals every day. And when it comes time for a younger generation to have another chance to enter the land, he's going to be there. Even though he'll be an old man, he'll be renewed as in his youth."

God's continuing purpose, the purpose that won't go away no matter what war, no matter what challenge, is: *The earth is going to be filled with the glory of the Lord.* China will be filled with the glory of the Lord. Russia will be filled with the glory of the Lord. The United States of America will be filled with the glory of the Lord. Yes, as truly as God lives, that will happen.

Selfishness Cannot Be Tolerated

After the years of wandering, the tribes of Reuben and Gad had large herds of livestock. They wanted to settle on the east side of the Jordan where there was good pasture, so they asked Moses not to take them across the Jordan. In Numbers 32:6

Moses answered, "Shall your brothers go to war while you yourselves sit here?"

We don't have to make evil happen; it's out there. We don't have to promote lies; they're out there. There is a war between good and evil. We have to face it, and if we retreat from it we'll end up nowhere. We know that God has an abiding moral purpose in the earth. So the provocative question is, "Shall your brothers go to war while you sit here?"

The question Moses asked these men is the one I want to ask you: "Will you sit here while other brothers and sisters go and fight your battle for you?" The question itself is an insult. To their great credit, the tribes of Reuben and Gad said, "No. We will cross over, and we will fight until the victory is won and there's rest for all." Selfishness did not destroy their will to enter into war.

Passivity Leads to Death

Passivity is a serious problem. In Numbers 33:50-53, 55-56 we read:

> Then the Lord spoke to Moses in the plains of Moab by the Jordan opposite Jericho, saying, "Speak to the sons of Israel and say to them, 'When you cross over the Jordan into the land of Canaan, then you shall drive out all the inhabitants of the land from before you, and destroy all their figured stones, and destroy all their molten images and demolish all their high places; and you shall take possession of the land and live in it, for I have given the land to you to possess it. [Remember that God owns all the earth. He can give it to whomever he wants and he can take it away from whomever he wants.] . . . But if you do not drive out the inhabitants of the land from before you, then it shall come about that those whom you let remain of them will become as pricks in your eyes and as thorns in your sides, and they

shall trouble you in the land in which you live. And it shall come about that as I plan to do to them, so I will do to you.'"

Did that happen? It sure did. Passivity had a high price. The pagan religions of the Canaanites infected the Israelites and caused all kinds of trouble. Ultimately, the Jews were driven from their land.

We Cannot Be Naive about the Power of Evil

Many people ask, "Why was God so prejudiced against these Canaanites? They were nice people, weren't they? Isn't it awful that the God of the Old Testament was for war and that he actually told the Israelites to hurt these people?"

Only those who are naive about the power of evil would ask these questions. The Amorites and the Moabites were born of incest. The Hittites and Canaanites worshiped Astarte (Ashtoreth) and Baal and Moloch. Their act of temple worship was prostitution, both female and male (homosexual prostitution). The statue of the god Moloch was a furnace; his belly was open, a fire was kindled inside, and his arms were stretched out. They took babies and laid them in his arms, and the babies rolled into the furnace as a sacrifice to their god.

God saw that and he said, "You don't have a right to have the land because the earth is mine and the fullness thereof. My glory shall fill it all. You don't have a right to it, so I'm taking it away from you."

Then God said to the Israelites, "You go in there as my children and as my servants who know the truth, and get them out of there! If you don't get them out of there, your children will begin to marry their children and act like their children, and you'll become tolerant of their gods. You'll soon be in their temple worshiping as they do, and I'll have to do to you what I did to them. You're special because of my purpose, and when you forget my purpose, you're not worth any more than they are. I'll have to raise up another people."

God said, "As truly as I live, all the earth shall be filled with my glory." Not with Americans, not with Southerners, not with Jews, not even with Christians—but with the glory of the Lord. And the people that will fill it with the glory of the Lord are those who pursue, preach, and live in the glory of the Lord.

Our secret is not in our past, not in our name, not in our culture. It's in our God! As long as we worship him and have the will to stand in his purpose, he will stand with us.

Procrastination Makes It Worse

There are other things that can sap our will to fight. In Joshua 18:3 we see that the issue of taking the land continues. Many battles had been fought, but Joshua had to say, "How long will you put off entering to take possession of the land which the Lord, the God of your fathers, has given you?"

How long are you going to procrastinate in taking what God told you to take? How much of your life will you let get away from you? The promises of God are not passively received. How long are you going to wait before taking them?

A friend of mine recently told me about going to the hospital and praying for a man who was near the end of his life. In the man's closing moments, he finally faced the issue of God's purpose in his life. Because he had put off confronting this all his life, he realized he had missed the benefits of so many of God's promises.

How long will you put off taking possession of what the Lord has for you? How long? As long as it takes for you to make up your mind to face it and, if necessary, to go to war for it. There's such a thing as a holy anger when you look at yourself in the mirror and say, "I'm not putting up with this procrastination anymore. It is ruining my life, and I'm going to do all that I can to see that it is defeated."

The Israelites had to learn to deal with the purposes of God. There was the generation that came up to Kadesh and *turned back*. Then the next generation crossed the Jordan *into* the land.

But now we're talking about a substantially different group years later who still hadn't taken *all* the land. Joshua was getting older himself, and he said, "How long are you going to wait to deal with this?"

R.G. Lee was a great man of God who preached until he was in his nineties. One of the greatest sermons I ever heard was in 1960 in Miami when he preached on the topic, "Lullaby, Alibi, and By-and-By": the lullaby attitude (everything's going to be all right), the alibi habit (always finding an excuse for defeat), and the by-and-by judgment (that will catch up to everyone). The question every group has to deal with, regardless of where they live or when they live, is, "Will we face the issues and deal with them before they destroy us?"

Difficulty Builds Character

Even though Israel failed to deal with the issue completely, God made use of the remnant of their enemies. In Judges 3:1-2, 4 we find this striking passage:

> Now these are the nations which the Lord left, to test Israel by them (that is, all who had not experienced any of the wars of Canaan; only in order that the generations of the sons of Israel might be taught war, those who had not experienced it formerly).... And they were for testing Israel, to find out if they would obey the commandments of the Lord, which He had commanded their fathers through Moses.

God left a few enemy tribes around to test the successive generations.

I talked to a man recently who said, "When I remember that my mother's parents took her to Oklahoma in a covered wagon when she was an infant, and when I realize what hardship she went through, I understand the strength that's in her spirit." Then he said, "How are we going to reproduce that in our offspring?" One of the great concerns I imagine most parents have is, "Will there be the right conditions to put mettle in the spirits of our children?"

I'm not suggesting that we get rid of all our conveniences. But the issue is, do we have the conditions that build strength of character in us and in our children? You don't build muscles without resistance. You don't build strength of character without enduring testing.

What we have inherited didn't come cheap, and it won't be maintained cheaply. Is it precious to you? Does it mean something to you? If it does, then you can't be passive about it. "All that is needed," said one great statesman, "for evil to triumph is for good men to do nothing." Do you have the will to enter the war? Weapons without will are of no use. Do you have the will? The man with the will is better off than the man with the weapon but without the will.

The will to war takes courage. This was the issue for Joshua when Moses died and passed on the mantle of leadership. After forty years of wandering, the Israelites were once again at the Jordan looking into the land. But forty years earlier Joshua, along with Caleb, had said, "We can do it! We can take the land!"—and nobody paid any attention. What would make the difference this time? What can we learn that Joshua learned when he faced the enemy in front of him with an unpredictable people behind him?

THREE

The Challenge to Be Courageous

A S WE LOOK AT THE FIRST CHAPTER of Joshua, consider the following:

—Does Joshua's leading the people of Israel into the Promised Land have any real implications for us today? Or is it simply a story of encouragement?
—How did the entrance of Joshua into the Promised Land influence the thinking of the apostles in the New Testament era?
—Are God's promises to be passively received or vigorously taken?
—What is *our* land of promise? Where is it?
—Are we settlers or pioneers?

The greatest heresy, in my opinion, is not a baptismal heresy, not a communion heresy, but rather is alluded to by James when he wrote, "Be ye doers of the word, and not hearers only, deceiving your own selves" (Jas 1:22 KJV). More people commit the heresy of "hearing without doing" than any other heresy in the world.

Consider, for example, the teaching and the life of the

apostle Paul. He was not reclusive; he was aggressive. He did not resign the claims of Christ over the earth—and because of him and those who were with him, many nations came to be ruled by Christ long, long ago. It has already been done. But there are generations who have allowed it to become undone by failing to attend to the Lord's business.

Against the backdrop of the claims of Christ and the preaching of the apostles, let's study the Book of Joshua and let it influence our thinking about what we're supposed to do on the earth. Joshua is a military book, a book about strategies and battles for land. It contains challenges, the first of which is the challenge to be courageous.

> Now it came about after the death of Moses the servant of the Lord that the Lord spoke to Joshua the son of Nun, Moses' servant, saying, "Moses My servant is dead; now therefore arise, cross this Jordan, you and all this people, to the land which I am giving to them, to the sons of Israel. Every place on which the sole of your foot treads, I have given it to you, just as I spoke to Moses. From the wilderness and this Lebanon, even as far as the great river, the river Euphrates, all the land of the Hittites, and as far as the Great Sea toward the setting of the sun, will be your territory. No man will be able to stand before you all the days of your life. Just as I have been with Moses, I will be with you; I will not fail you or forsake you." (Jos 1:1-5)

The word *courage* means to be battle-ready in spirit, to be vigorous. It's an active word, not a passive word. It means to be vigilant, alert, poised to spring into action.

Whenever I give a teaching about a word, I look it up in the dictionary—a Noah Webster 1828 edition. Noah Webster was a born-again Christian, and my edition has his testimony in the front of it. He speaks of his conversion and of being led by the Holy Spirit to write the dictionary. Frequently his dictionary gives biblical definitions and cites scriptural passages. I looked up the word *courage* in this dictionary, and the word comes from the French word for "heart," and it means "to have heart." Courage is the quality that enables us to face danger and difficulty with firmness and without fear or depression.

Then Webster cites Deuteronomy 31, where Moses is laying hands on Joshua and telling him to have courage. So I went to Webster for a definition of courage and he sent me back to Joshua. In Joshua we have probably the best biblical definition of a person who was called to be courageous. We need to see that call to be courageous in the light of his mission to take the land. We cannot take the land and obtain God's promises without dealing with the issue of courage—that is, to be spiritually vigilant, alert, ready to spring into action, able to face danger (real danger, if we're talking about real promises) with firmness, and without fear or depression.

The Courage to Lead

The name *Moses* means "drawn out"—he was drawn out of the waters, and he drew Israel out of Egypt. Moses was one of the greatest men who ever lived. Raised in the palace as Pharaoh's grandson, he had the best education that the world offered in his day, every advantage. He was royalty!

But even though he had everything that the most powerful nation on the earth had to offer, he saw that his natural people had nothing; they were enslaved, abused, victims of all kinds of injustice, under the whiplash of his adopted people. When he saw the plight of his natural people, he made the choice to identify with them. He chose "to suffer affliction with the people of God, rather than to enjoy the pleasures of sin for a season" (Heb 11:25 KJV). He left the palace and became a pioneer.

He chose to identify with Israel, took this race of slaves and made them a people. It was under his leadership that God called them a holy nation. He's the one who made them a covenant people and bound them together according to covenant promises which God had already given to Abraham. He gave them their law and constitution by divine revelation. He was their prophet and chief spokesman. In effect, he was their monarch because he had absolute power, and as their military commander he won many battles.

But even Moses was challenged when it was time to lead. Perhaps he stammered, perhaps he lisped, but when the Holy Spirit spoke to him and said, "I want you to be a leader," he answered, "I can't talk." Every man that God uses has to face his own weakness. If a man doesn't face it, he has no business leading because he grossly underestimates what's required. Moses faced his weakness, and subsequently his disciple, the man he had trained for forty years, Joshua, had to face his own weakness, also.

Joshua the Man

Joshua means "deliverance"—"God's salvation." *Joshua* actually means the same thing as *Jesus.* At this point in history he was God's salvation for the Jews. He was their deliverer, the one who would bring them into the land.

Consider the relationship between Moses and Joshua. Joshua was not palace-trained. He did not have the advantages of an Egyptian education. Everything he knew, everything he was, Moses had taught him.

He was not only trained by Moses but he was probably also named by Moses because it was normal for a master to name his disciple. Jesus renamed several of his disciples, and it was not uncommon at all for a teacher to rename a disciple according to his character or his mission.

Forty years earlier Joshua was one of the twelve men who spied out the land, and he and Caleb brought back a "good report." They said it was possible to go into the land, but the others had said it was not, and the "evil report" prevailed. But Joshua stayed committed to God's purpose for forty years. At the end of forty years, he was still committed to the vision that God had given to his spiritual leader. When his leader died, he was still committed to carrying it out, "even as the Lord spoke to Moses."

Do you notice the rank? Joshua 1:1 says, ". . . after the death of Moses *the servant of the Lord*. . . the Lord spoke to Joshua . . . *Moses' servant.* . . ." He was considered a servant, yet he was coming into leadership.

Most of us who are leaders have had people that we've looked up to; they towered above us. I remember I drove a thousand miles to hear Dr. R.G. Lee preach, and if I had to do it over again, I'd drive another thousand miles. I stood on my feet one night for an hour and a half listening to him preach—it seemed like fifteen minutes. I was enthralled and spellbound by this great man of God. I've also driven great distances to hear W.A. Crisswell of the First Baptist Church of Dallas preach. He had a great influence on me when I was a young man looking for a leader to emulate and learn from.

But the day comes when we must stand and we must lead. We must face an issue in ourselves that takes more courage than anything else: we have to deal with who we are and whether we're up to the job that God has called us to do.

"Moses Is Dead, Joshua!"

The first message that Joshua gets as a new leader—and in those days it was the first message that most leaders ever got because they didn't become leaders until this happened—is, "Moses is dead."

This is more than a statement of fact; this is a statement of responsibility. How would you like to have to believe God out in the wilderness for the daily food and water for two to three million people and all their sheep and goats? How would you like to be on the brink of bringing this people into the land they'd once rejected, especially if you'd had a firsthand, upclose look at what leadership had done to your predecessor?

"Moses is dead, Joshua!" Among the implications is that the past is past; it's over with. The past was wonderful; it was the beginning of covenant. It was the time of the law and the

Pentateuch. But Moses is dead. Some people can never turn loose of the past; they don't have the courage to. Therefore they're never quite ready to deal with what's ahead.

Another implication of Moses' death is that the buck now stops with Joshua. Up until that point, whenever people got into a fight and came to Joshua and said, "We're having a problem here," he'd say, "I'm seeing Moses this afternoon; I'll get back to you." Or he'd say, "Moses said . . ." and it would carry weight because Moses said it. But he couldn't do that anymore. Today Moses' tent was vacant and *he* had to have the answers. The implications of this settled on Joshua like a landslide.

"Take the Land, Joshua!"

The second message he gets is, "Arise, take these people across Jordan and take the land that's been promised to them." The difficult thing is that there isn't much time between these two messages. They're in the same verse, as it were. Joshua didn't have thirty days to mourn for a great leader who was past and then to go through all his notes to be sure he knew what he was doing. It all came at once. "Moses is dead—you're the new leader. And your first job is to get them across the river." There's no word yet about how he was supposed to do that. God just told Joshua, "You take all these people across that river"—which, incidentally, was at flood stage—"and get them over there on the other side, and then drive out all the enemies." If I were in Joshua's shoes, I might have said, "Well, you can forget the rest of it until we get the first part figured out, Lord." It seemed an insurmountable mission that God gave to him.

Facing the Issues

There were two issues that faced Joshua—and that in some sense face every leader. They were things that he had to keep in perspective in order to fulfill God's call: how he got where he was and where he was going next.

1. Keeping the faith. The first issue is: *Be faithful to the heritage.* We may be innovative and creative, but we can't break the faith with those who brought us this far. Every leader has to deal with the issue of keeping the faith. "Follow Moses and be faithful to your heritage. Moses is dead, but you are built on, trained by, committed to the vision that was given to Moses."

2. Accomplish the objectives. The second issue is: *Be faithful to the same purpose that God gave to Moses.* Obtain God's promises! Every leader has to be faithful to his heritage, but he also has to push forward to obtain the objectives.

Behind us is a foundation, but in front of us is a mission. Moses had finished his course, and the leaders who have preceded us, our fathers and mothers and the saints of old, have finished their course and they have kept the faith, but our course remains in front of us. We must be faithful to the past, and we must be faithful to the high calling which is before us.

This is a wonderful promise: "I've given you Moses and I'm giving you the land. Now get on and get with it."

"Who Made You a Leader Over Us?"

God spoke to Moses when he was at the burning bush: "Moses, I will deliver my people from their terrible task-masters and give them a good and spacious land, flowing with milk and honey. And I'm sending you to see that it gets done." What a beautiful promise! In doing the will of God, Moses faced some problems, and if you are called to lead, you'll meet them, too.

1. First, not everybody wants you to lead them. Ever notice that? There are some people who weren't there when God told you to lead. They don't know you're supposed to lead them, and that's one reason why we need courage. Usually it's not the ones who know you're supposed to lead them that will try your courage.

Have you ever felt God lead you to someone who didn't want what you had to give? It's not a good feeling. When I was first beginning to travel and speak at conferences, I went with a minister friend who was ministering at a conference. He was an Englishman and had graduated from Cambridge University, Eaton College. He spoke with a dignified accent, and at this stage of his ministry he was sometimes less than tactful, though spiritually perceptive. In this particular meeting, he was speaking very eloquently. Now I've found that people usually want to be ministered to by the person who has preached. That's true even when everything else is equal. But not only was I unknown by the people at the conference, I'm also from Southern Alabama, so my accent indicated to them a serious intelligence gap between him and me.

After the meeting, we went into the prayer room and he said to me, "I want you to help me pray for these people."

I said, "All right," and went over to a dignified lady in her middle forties and asked, "Would you like me to pray for you?"

She said, "No, I'm waiting for the other minister."

I felt rejected and I thought: *Sister, I hope you have to wait a long time.* I had been all ready to help her; my spirit had risen up within me, and she had just jammed it right back down.

I went to him and said, "I'd like to pray for her, but she wants *you* to pray for her."

He understood right away, so he went over to her in all his dignity and severity and said, "What's the problem?"

She said, "My husband can't stand me."

"Well, I can understand that," he retorted. Poor woman.

As he turned away, she looked at me with her mascara dripping onto her blouse, and she said, "Would *you* pray for me?"

I said, "Of course I'll pray for you."

You see, there are times when people don't want *you* to lead them. But that's not the only problem.

2. *Those already in the land don't necessarily want it taken from them.* Your enemies don't appreciate your mission statement,

and if you put on your letterhead, "I have come to take the land," they will send your mail back to you. They don't understand that the land is yours, and some of them will put up a fight.

God gave Israel a land; he's given the church the earth. We must deal with the world. It takes courage to lead because we will face some people who don't want our leadership and others who don't want us to conquer what they are standing on. But we must do it because the Lord has called us to do it.

The Courage to Achieve Our Objectives

The courage to take on the job is just the first step. The next step is the courage to achieve our objectives.

> "Be strong and courageous, for you shall give this people possession of the land which I swore to their fathers to give them. Only be strong and very courageous; . . . Have I not commanded you? Be strong and courageous! Do not tremble or be dismayed, for the Lord your God is with you wherever you go." (Jos 1:6, 7a, 9)

I like the last line, "for the Lord your God is with you wherever you go." The end result is summed up in Revelation 12:11: "And they overcame him because of the blood of the Lamb and because of the word of their testimony, and they did not love their life even to death."

The challenge is to have the courage to achieve our objectives. If we'll listen, there is a mission statement in our call. God doesn't just call us, he calls us *to do something,* and if we'll listen a little longer, he'll tell us just exactly what it is. God's not trying to figure it out; he knows what he wants us to do, and he calls us to do just that. We need to be courageous, therefore, to do what God has called us to do, whatever it is, to achieve the objective. It's out there in front of us.

God called Joshua. Of course, Joshua's task was a little

harder than most tasks. If we take our call literally, it will be a literal challenge. God's in the ground-taking business—neighborhoods, cities, real things.

Three times God tells Joshua to be courageous. When God says something once we should take note. But three times? When God says, "I have something for you to do, and I want you to be *courageous*"—that's a clue!

We say, "I always wanted to serve you, Lord."

"Well, I have something for you to do. Are you courageous?"

"Uh, is there anything else you have for me to do?"

He hasn't even said what it is yet, but we have a clue! Then he says, "Yes, I do have something for you to do. I want you to be strong and *very* courageous."

"Well, just being courageous had me nervous."

But God goes farther: "I want you to be strong, and courageous, *and* I don't want you to be terrified."

"Terrified Lord? I wasn't scared at all until you started telling me how to get ready for this job!"

Be Strong to Take the Land

I was called to Mobile, Alabama. I've been in that area since I was six years old. Mobile, Alabama, is not the place where everybody ought to be, but God called *me* there. It's the hardest place in the world for me to be because I made most of my mistakes in Mobile—except those that I made on the road—and I have to live with them. I'm more controversial in Mobile, Alabama, than I am anywhere in the world. A lot of my ministry is traveling; I could live traveling. But God called me to Mobile, and I love that place because God put it in my heart.

I'm not the only man of God there, but I'm one of the men of God there and I know the spiritual principality over that city. I know him. In fact, we know each other well. I know what I must deal with in that city. I believe that Jesus Christ is Lord of Mobile, Alabama.

I believe he's also Lord of New Orleans, and New York, and Chicago, and Portland. I believe he's Lord of wherever you are. God put you there to take that land. God put you there to manifest the Kingdom of God—righteousness, peace, and joy in the Holy Spirit. You're there to take the land! You're not there to make peace with the enemy or to make an accommodation with him. You're there to bring the glory of the Lord into that area.

I realize this is radical, but I believe it. While the full manifestation of Christ's kingdom awaits his appearing and our immortality, he does rule in and through us now.

Jesus wants to redeem people; he doesn't want to damn them. He wants to use his people for redemption. We need, therefore, to worship him in their presence. We need to break evil forces and show the nations the glory of God. We need to call upon the nations to accept Jesus Christ as the Lord and King of creation—because he is. Our mission takes courage.

Do you believe that God will spread his influence and his power and authority through your area? We are the light of the world, the city set on a hill, the salt of the earth. We need to be aggressive. We need to have the courage to take the land.

Joshua wasn't standing by the river waiting for an escape. He was looking for the way to get over to the other side so he could deal with the enemy.

"Be courageous and take the land!" We don't just passively wait to receive the land, we *obtain* the promises of God. Maybe we don't have the whole city as our mission; maybe we just have a few blocks. But whatever God has given us, take it, rule it, and glorify God in it. Manifest his righteousness, peace, and joy.

Courage to Confront the Enemy

God told Joshua, "When you look at your enemies, don't shake!" (see Jos 1:9). We're not allowed to show fear in the army of God.

In recent years, people have been encouraged to let their

emotions hang out all over. We're "touchy-feely." But in Bible-times and later, people were more stoic. Good soldiers don't "let it all hang out." When the enemy growls and roars, a good soldier just looks at him like he's a butterfly.

The enemy loves to growl and roar because he's an intimidator. But if you're the kind of Christian who's being talked about here, you'll roar right back. The enemy says, "Hey, I've been around to six churches and roaring always works. Why isn't it working on you? What kind of Christian are you?"

And you'll say, "I'm a mean Christian, and if you don't stop growling, I'll bite *you*!"

Don't be terrorized. The enemy can't terrorize people who won't be terrorized. Scripture says, "They loved not their life to death" (Rev 12:11). Courageous people can't be scared out of the will of God.

I used to have a terrible fear of the IRS. Any correspondence that had IRS in the return address corner caused my heart to skip two beats. Then our church went through a long audit. By the time it was over—and by the grace of God our records were sufficiently accurate that we did not have to pay anything and were not guilty of anything!—the three-year battle delivered me from my fears.

Whatever you're afraid of, you must deal with it. I'm not talking about *bravado* or *braggadocio*. I'm talking about con-fronting the enemy without showing fear. If you're afraid, the enemy will sniff out your fear. So face your fear. Let God deal with it. Don't be terrorized. "If any man draw back, my soul shall have no pleasure in him" (Heb 10:38, KJV).

FOUR

The Challenge to Inspire Courage

YOU MUST HAVE COURAGE, but you also have to *inspire courage* in others because you can't take the land by yourself. You want your people to have courage because you need them to take the land with you.

Joshua was not only courageous, he was also able to make his people courageous. When Joshua finished speaking to them, they said, "Let's go!" A leader can inspire courage but, of course, he can't do it if he doesn't have it himself. If you have courage—and God can give us all courage because courage comes from him—and if you begin to inspire courage in your people, they'll be with you in the battle.

The Courage to Inspire Others to Act

It's very tempting to talk about the land, to analyze the situation, to size up the giants, to weigh the pros and cons—and never really do anything about taking the land. But if we "keep the faith" with a clear idea of the action that got us here and keep our eye on where we're going, eventually a generation will arise that will say, "We are with you to take the land."

Inspiration changes the odds. I've watched and played sports all my life. I've seen a poor team get inspired and a good team fall flat. If you get your people inspired, who knows what they might do?

Once I gave my dad a German Shepherd dog because he was being harassed by neighborhood prowlers. He kept the dog behind a chainlink fence. One day some fellows came by and taunted the dog. My dad came out of the house and said to them, "Now, you don't want to do that because that dog can jump the fence; he just doesn't know it yet."

The devil has taunted the church. The "fences" are there, but the church can jump the fences if it gets inspired. The church can do far more than it ever dreamed it could do because we're in relationship with a God who can do all things. But we need to inspire our people.

George Washington and George Patton are measured not so much by the courage they had, but by the courage they inspired in their followers. They were men of action, not mere analyzers.

Watch out for analysis paralysis. Israel was commanded to act, not analyze. Israel had analyzed things forty years earlier and had turned their backs on the challenge. But:

> Then Joshua commanded the officers of the people, saying, "Pass through the midst of the camp and command the people, saying, 'Prepare provisions for yourselves, for within three days you are to cross this Jordan, to go in to possess the land which the Lord your God is giving you, to possess it.'" (Jos 1:10, 11)

God's people need to be structured for action. We are not a holy mob; we are a holy nation. We are bound together in the purposes of God to do the will of God. The relationships and life of the church need to be ordered in such a way as to allow the people to obtain objectives, so that when the leaders hear from God, the people can be rallied and inspired to act.

Don't be a "simulator church." If you were ever to become a jet pilot, you'd probably train on a *simulator*. I don't know much about flying or simulators, but as I understand it, it's just like an airplane inside. You get in, close the door, and for all intents and purposes you're inside an airplane. It has the same buttons and knobs, levers and dials that an airplane has. In front of you is a screen that makes it appear that you're actually controlling an airplane. You can take off, you can bank right, you can bank left, you can climb, you can even crash. You experience motion and gravity. It's a simulation of the real thing.

You feel as though you're flying. You can "fly" a long time and seem to go a long distance. But when you land and climb out, you're right where you were when you got in.

I've visited simulator churches. You go in, close the door behind you, and you feel like you're moving. You can feel yourself taking off, and you're climbing high; you feel like you've done great things. If the speaker is good, he can make you feel that you're really going places. You vicariously experience his descriptive message, without ever wrinkling your Sunday clothes. However, when you step out of the door on Sunday morning, you're right where you were when you went in.

Simulation can become deception if it's a permanent way of life. Can you imagine a poor soul who rented time in a simulator on the belief that he was actually traveling?

Wandering around is much like simulators. You feel like you are going somewhere but you are not. Wandering is a curse. If God wants to curse someone, he makes him a wanderer. God said, "Cain, I'm going to curse you because you murdered your brother. You're a wanderer. From now on you'll just wander around. Anyone who sees you will say, 'Uh, oh, there's Cain. See the mark on him? He cannot stay here—he's a wanderer.'"
Later God said to Israel, "Because you would not go into the

land, you will be a wandering people. You'll just wander around for forty years"—a long, unnecessary journey.

A pastor friend, Houston Miles, once said, "A fanatic is someone who, when he loses his sense of direction, redoubles his efforts." That's also what wandering is like. Lots of effort with no direction.

You ask, "But how do I know if we're going somewhere or not?" Well, if you've been around there often before, the chances are that you are wandering.

The Courage to Stay on Course

A frequent problem among churches and Christians is that they lack courage to keep going forward, and end up going in circles. My friend Ern Baxter says, "Lost men go in circles." God warned Joshua to stay on course and keep the law:

> "... be careful to do according to all the law which Moses My servant commanded you; do not turn from it to the right or to the left, so that you may have success wherever you go. This book of the law shall not depart from your mouth, but you shall meditate on it day and night, so that you may be careful to do according to all that is written in it; for then you will make your way prosperous, and then you will have success." (Jos 1:7b, 8)

It takes courage to stay on course and keep the rules. We can't deviate from directions—nor the ways of God—to get to the goal. His rules serve his purpose.

I'll make a confession: I love football. I like to watch the bowl games, but one of the most miserable experiences I ever had was December, 1985, when Alabama played Southern California.

I had the TV tray up with all kinds of goodies on it, and my feet were propped up on the easy chair. It was to be a special day. The telephones were turned off, the family was all in order, and the house was full of righteousness, peace, and joy. Leaning back in my easy chair, I had a better seat than anybody in the stadium.

Southern Cal and Alabama are both great schools and have great football traditions. Players and fans were ready. They'd been eating raw steaks for weeks, bench pressing until their muscles had muscles, and running plays until they could do it in their sleep. Some linemen weighed 280 pounds and some 310 pounds—they were big and fast. Everybody was fine tuned, and I was expecting *action*.

The players were lined up across the field, pawing at the ground. Veins were sticking out on their necks. They were serious. You could feel it.

After the kick off return, the teams lined up on the line of scrimmage. Just as the play started, somebody in the back field moved early. Just a little nervous twitch, then the fellow in a striped uniform came out—he didn't weigh over 150 pounds. He was not a mean looking fellow, but he blew his little whistle—*tweet! tweet!*—and everything stopped—players, cheerleaders, fans, TV audience—everything. Four thousand pounds of manpower on that line froze right there, and the little fellow in the striped uniform picked up the ball and started walking back, fifteen yards!

"Well," I thought, "I'll get over that. Now, referee, you get off the field, so we can have a *game*." The team went back in a huddle and got all charged up again. They were all ready to go—then that little fellow blew his whistle again and came running up and grabbed the ball. They had taken too long in the huddle! It looked like he was going to walk clear out of the stadium with the ball. I thought, "What is going on here? They came to play ball and this fellow thinks it's *his ball!*" I was out of my chair and down in front of the set, yelling, "Get off the field! Get off! There are millions of fans trying to watch a game and you're ruining it!"

For the whole first half, my team went backwards more than they went forwards. All the coaches were pulling their hair out.

Somebody was doing something wrong on every play, jumping, lurching, all out of rhythm. I kept thinking, "If it weren't for that referee . . ."

But, it wasn't the referee that penalized them; they penalized themselves.

It was so much like the church, I had to quit watching. We get trained, know all the Bible verses, pray up a storm, bind every demon; we're ready to go! Then somebody breaks the rules and the whole team's walking backwards.

When I was young I thought rules were for weak people. If you weren't courageous, you kept the rules; but if you really had nerve, if you were brave and strong, you didn't mind breaking a few rules.

I found out it takes a lot more courage to keep the rules than it does to break them. God didn't give us the rules to obstruct us; the rules are there to make us successful. If we break the rules, we don't win the game. Paul said, "He does not win the prize unless he competes according to the *rules*" (2 Tm 2:5).

It takes courage to keep God's rules. We can't say, "Well, the end justifies the means, and we should go for it any way we can"—run over one another, mistreat one another, have a spirit of competition, lie or be dishonest, anything to obtain the objective. We can't do that! We have to obtain our objectives, but we must have the courage to do it *right*. God will honor us if we do it according to his laws.

As a man who used many athletic metaphors, Paul once said, "I don't fight as a man who misses" (1 Cor 9:26 paraphrased). In other words, "When I throw a punch, it *lands*." We need to make our punches land. We need to discipline our bodies, our spirits, and our minds, so that we can win the crown, so that we can achieve our goals, so that we can stop penalizing ourselves. The courage to keep the rules will keep us moving forward.

The Courage to Keep God's People Together

Joshua not only had to inspire courage in the people to act. He not only had to help the people understand that their success depended on doing all that God had commanded. He also faced the challenge of keeping the flock together. Here's what happened:

Our goals are not personal goals. Remember those two and a half tribes who wanted to settle on the east bank? They came to Moses just before he died and said, "Moses, this land on the east side of the Jordan is nice land. We've been looking at it and it's good for our livestock." They used these words: "Do not take us across the Jordan" (Nm 32:5).

Remember Moses' response? "What do you mean?" he said. "You're doing exactly what your fathers did forty years ago. Why are you discouraging your brothers? *Will you sit here while your brothers go to war?*"

They answered, "Well, no."

Moses said, "All right. I'll give you the land if you'll go over with your brothers and fight with them until they enter their rest and then you can come back." So they agreed to do that.

When Joshua assumed command and it was time to cross the Jordan, the leaders of these two and a half tribes reminded him of the promise Moses had made. "Moses promised us we could have this land." The key to fulfilling our personal goals is maintaining corporate life and purpose.

Joshua said, "Moses also charged you to go and fight with your brothers until they come into their rest. If you will go over with them, you can have this land." The key to fulfilling our personal goals is maintaining corporate life and purpose.

We cannot rejoice in personal success when there is corporate failure. We cannot be satisfied to bring our own flock into its rest while the Body of Christ languishes. Our goals are not personal goals. They are corporate goals.

The high cost of complaining and division. The pledge these men made to Joshua was, "We will stay together until the work is done." In the last few verses of Joshua 1, they say soberly, "If anybody rebels against you, we will kill them" (see Jos 1:18).

That's a shocking statement but this was a new generation, made up of people who had been under twenty years old when the first generation had their opportunity to enter the land. For forty years they had buried their parents and older brothers and sisters by the thousands—daily. As they wandered from place to place, imagine the children often asking their parents, "Why don't we get out of the wilderness?" And always receiving the same reply: "We had a chance. There was a time we could have, but we rebelled. We murmured and complained, and when we heard about the enemies we turned back and brought a curse on ourselves. We have to stay out here. We can't go back to Egypt because they'll kill us, and we can't go into the land because they'll kill us, and God won't help us. God's angry with us, and we'll die out here in the wilderness."

They heard that story so many times that they thought, "If murmuring caused this, it's a terrible thing and should never be allowed again."

Their conclusion was: "If we ever have the chance again to enter the land, we will not turn back," so they made a rule that if murmuring started in the camp, there would be an execution, because they did not want to wander anymore. As they thought about their heritage, they understood what had happened: A whole generation of people had talked themselves out of the purposes of God.

Their penalty for murmuring was hard, but not nearly as hard as the result that unchecked murmuring caused the entire nation. The murmuring and the division had killed not one or two murmurers but a whole generation of Israelites. They recognized that murmuring is malignant.

If we intend to take the land today, we have to stay together. If we're going to stay together, we have to stop murmuring. We have to understand the price that it exacts from us. The church has talked itself out of God's promises too often. Every time we talk about how impossible his plan is, every time we talk about the odds against us, every time we talk about how bad it's getting, every time we talk about depressing news and dwell on it, every time we talk about how frail we are—we're talking ourselves out of the promise. Every time we talk about the problems of other Christians and belabor the faults of other groups, dealing out division on the right and on the left—we're talking ourselves out of the promise because we need the whole church in order to take the land.

You can apply these principles in this book in many ways to your own life and to your local church—the courage to lead, the courage to go for your objectives, the courage to confront your enemies, the courage to inspire others, the courage to keep the rules, the courage to keep the group together—but we need to apply it to the larger Body of Christ.

If you have been called to lead and that calling has been tested and confirmed, then don't give up just because you encounter opposition from a few. Set God-given goals to inspire your people and keep them marching together.

Banish discouragement. We don't usually think of discouragement as a lack of courage. However, if you say, "I had courage, but I got discouraged," that simply means that your courage was taken away from you.

When I get in a testing situation, I pray a little prayer that God gave me—I pray according to my calling: "God, the ministry was never my idea to start with, it was yours. You called me; I know that you did; I've never doubted it. But *if you called me*"—I say this not because I doubt it, but because it transfers the responsibility to God—"it's your turn, Lord. I've done all I can do; now you have to do something."

I don't use that prayer lightly. When I'm in a situation where I can't do anything else, God will answer. If you're discouraged, if you've come up against a wall of resistance, I believe God will do something on your behalf. If you know God called you, stand on that fact. If he called you, you have his authority, his power, his resources. Defer to the Holy Spirit.

Are you thinking about getting away from the problem, trying to escape from it instead of dealing with it? Every man, every woman, who serves God has had to deal with this at one time or another. You want to get away; it's overwhelming! You think, "If I could just go away somewhere!"

Listen: turn your face into the problem.

I fought one night with the desire to escape until the bed was wet with perspiration. I wanted to catch a bus to anywhere. I lay there with a fever and sore throat, sick in body as well as soul. I'd become discouraged; something had hurt me, grieved me, and I wanted to leave. It hadn't been my idea to be a preacher in the first place. I said, "I want out, Lord!" It was two o'clock in the morning, I didn't have anywhere to turn for help, and suddenly God said, "Confess your faith." For fifteen minutes, I confessed everything I could think of that I believed. I continued until I felt the Spirit of God anoint me, and I began to weep.

Then I had a vision. I saw a man, dressed like one of David's warriors, one of his mighty men. He had on leather sandals, and in his hand he had a sword. He was a rugged looking character standing in a field of vegetables. He was shouting to a group of people around the field, "You can't have this field! You can't have this field!" There was a rhythm to it, and I began to say it with him: "You can't have this field! You can't have this field!"

At that point, God said to me, "Don't give up what I've given you." I jumped out of bed, grabbed my Bible, and opened it to the very page where the story of Shammah is written (2 Sam 23:11, 12). I knew it was from God and I began to say: "Devil, you can't have this field."

Put your face to it; there's a way through. You don't have to try to find a way *out*; there's a way *through*. Banish discouragement in the name of the Lord. A bruised reed he will not break, a smoldering wick he will not put out. God can give you the victory you need.

FIVE

Know the Enemy

G OD'S PROMISES ARE GRACIOUS and receiving them is so fulfilling. It's necessary, however, to deal with the fact that between us and the grapes of God's grace are the giants of opposition. God's Word teaches that we are to know our enemy. We must not be ignorant of the enemy's devices. We can't afford to ignore or underestimate the enemy. The greatest danger is not that the enemy will overpower us; it is that we will be ignorant and deceived. There's nothing that makes us more vulnerable than the arrogance of ignorance. I believe God wants us to have a right understanding about the evil we are dealing with. Let's not be so wrapped up in our own limited perspective and pride that we fail to be willing to spy out the enemy.

Behind Enemy Lines

In Joshua 2 we see how Joshua dealt with ignorance as he sent out a little "reckon" patrol:

> Then Joshua the son of Nun sent two men as spies secretly from Shittim, saying, "Go, view the land, especially Jericho." So they went and came into the house of a harlot

whose name was Rahab, and lodged there. And it was told the king of Jericho, saying, "Behold, men from the sons of Israel have come here tonight to search out the land." And the king of Jericho sent word to Rahab, saying, "Bring out the men who have come to you, who have entered your house, for they have come to search out all the land." But the woman had taken the two men and hidden them, and she said, "Yes, the men came to me, but I did not know where they were from. And it came about when it was time to shut the gate, at dark, that the men went out; I do not know where the men went. Pursue them quickly, for you will overtake them." But she had brought them up to the roof and hidden them in the stalks of flax which she had laid in order on the roof. So the men pursued them on the road to the Jordan to the fords; and as soon as those who were pursuing them had gone out, they shut the gate. (Jos 2: 1-7)

The mission of the two spies was very simple: "Go, view the land, especially Jericho." Thank God for simple directions, and thank God for people who can carry out simple directions.

Simple, but not easy. These spies did not have the Book of Joshua to help them with a plan of action: "We don't really know where to go, so let's turn to the Book of Joshua and see." But who would have believed that God would lead them into the house of a harlot?

The Israelites were camped on the east side of the Jordan Valley, which is about twelve miles wide. The river ran down the middle of the valley. Jericho was situated across the river and almost up against the other hillside. These spies had to cross the valley and the river, which was at flood stage, then begin the long walk toward Jericho, hiding as they went along.

The Significance of the Objective

"Jericho" means city of fragrance. It was an oasis with beautiful palms. Physically speaking, it was a lovely place to live. It was also a fort and a place of great military significance because Jericho was approximately in the middle of the land of Canaan, north and south. So there was a strategic military significance in taking Jericho first because that would divide the whole country in half, the Canaanites would be split in two, and the local tribes would be thrown into disarray. And that is precisely what happened.

The Nature of the Objective

Jericho was a citadel; it was a fortress; it was the place that had to be taken first before the Israelites could get the rest of their promises. It was an obstruction, guarding the Promised Land. It was as though hell itself had built this citadel. To attack it was like storming the gates of hell. It was the place where the enemy had a fortified position so that no one could get in and take the land. Yet it was the very place God led the Israelites to first.

God knows what he's doing! God leads you to the very place where he wants you to sit. He will bring you face to face with the very obstacle that you must overcome. If you defeat that one, the rest of the opposition begins to crumble. This was one of those situations.

The Need for Discretion

I don't think we should be afraid of the enemy, but we should have sober respect for the enemy. Sometimes we get cocky. For instance, I love a powerful meeting. I love a meeting that gets me so inspired that I feel like I could go out and beat the devil single-handedly. But I have to realize that I am not wrestling with flesh and blood but with powers and principalities and spiritual wickedness in high places. If I become arrogant, I can sometimes pick more of a fight with the devil than I know what to do with. I need to keep my task and my calling in perspective and not boast beyond my measure.

For example, a fellow came to me the other day who had quite a few problems. He had traced a lot of his misery back to a large meeting when he got up publicly and tried to bind the evil spiritual powers over all of America. I told him, "You probably should have started with a little town somewhere out in the country."

Years ago I was looking at boats. The agent showed me a large boat that could be bought cheap. It was beautiful but way too big for me. The name of the boat was "Arrogant." It had a small dinghy on board named "Cocky." When I asked why it was for sale, he said the owner was in trouble with the I.R.S. "No wonder," I thought. "With names like that, trouble is inevitable."

The Need for Knowledge

Many world leaders throughout various periods of history had no idea what really was going on in the world. Therefore they underestimated their enemies. However, Winston Churchill was one of the few men in the early 1930s who understood what was going on. That was long before he really came to international prominence, and most of his fellow members of Parliament thought he was eccentric and odd. But he understood that Adolf Hitler was a force with which the world would have to reckon. He understood that a war was coming. If the rest of the world had understood it earlier, we might have saved a lot of bloodshed, but Western Europe and the U.S. were ignorant of the enemy's devices.

In suggesting that we must come to grips with what really holds power in the world—ideologically and spiritually—and what God wants to do about it, I'm not saying that we should become preoccupied with the enemy. But, we need to have a realistic view of the spiritual forces that oppose us and respect them for what they are. Preoccupation will lead to fear, but perception will lead us to prepare and protect.

Understand the Enemy's Weak Points

One antidote to fear is to ask God to show us the enemy's weak points. My football coach used to say, "Boys, don't be afraid of the opponent. Respect him, but don't be afraid of him. The other team doesn't hang their trousers on the wall and jump in them. They put them on one leg at a time, just like you do."

In addition to knowing the strengths of the enemy, we must also discover its weaknesses, its vulnerable points, where it is decaying and ready to crumble from within.

Internal Corruption

The religion of Jericho was Canaanite. As I mentioned before, there were three principal gods and goddesses. Baal was the god of earthly fertility, a male god. Astarte (Ashtoreth) was the goddess of fertility, the sex goddess. In the temples of Baal and Astarte prostitution was part of the worship. Perhaps Rahab, who is mentioned in Joshua 2, was actually one of these temple prostitutes. The third in this triad was Moloch, the god of fire. His image was a furnace. Many times the children conceived as a result of prostitution in the temples of Astarte and Baal were sacrificed into the arms of the furnace of Moloch and burned alive. The practice of the worshipers of Astarte, Baal, and Moloch was to enjoy sex, but to reject the fruit and responsibility. Also, homes were often dedicated by putting a newborn child in an urn and sealing it up and burying it under the doorpost of the house.

I believe that God rejected the Canaanites because of their corruption. God owns the land. God can give it and God can take it away. People do not own anything; it is only loaned to them by the mercies of God. He had allowed these tribes to occupy this land, but because of their spiritual and physical adultery, he was going to take it away from them. In order to purge the land, he sent the Israelites in.

We cannot imagine the sexually transmitted diseases that were rampant in the Hittite and Canaanite cultures because of their religious practices. But they would approximate, I imagine, the sort of diseases that plague our own society. We cannot imagine the sorrow that came with the sacrifice of babies and the cheapened value of life. All false religion is a product of hell, but false religion is usually not satisfied just to be wrong; it must also oppress. The enemy, whenever he gains the attention and worship of people, becomes a terrible oppressor. The only liberation for it is by the power of God.

Weighed Down with Guilt

When people are involved in gross wickedness, they are vulnerable to the forces of righteousness. In spite of all their bravado, it seems they know there is cause to fear God. The people in Jericho were aware of the Israelites across the river. They had spies of their own, and so the city was locked up tight at night. They were very nervous about what was going on.

When the Israelites discovered the fear in the city of Jericho, it gave them an edge. We can benefit, too, by a little reconnaissance. Instead of becoming emotional, try to understand calmly what you are dealing with. Spy it out. Read about it. Look at it. Ask God for the key to unlock it and see it as a means to higher goals and higher ends. Look beyond your Jericho to a land that's stretching out before you.

Don't take the path of least resistance. I used to feel sorry for myself when I was in a struggle until I realized that that's a sign of God's love. The path of least resistance makes men and rivers crooked. No one ever drifted to success.

If God loves you enough to put obstacles before you, he is dealing with you as a son or a daughter.

Do Not Glorify the Enemy

It is easy to get sidetracked, especially when we are talking about the enemy. It is easy either to underestimate and pay no attention or to get carried away in a manner that glorifies the enemy. But, we have a promised prize, and we have the weapons for our warfare that God has given to us. We have the blood of Jesus Christ. We must not build up the enemy in our own eyes or the eyes of others.

For instance, I believe that Marxism is already judged. While it may cause great harm in the lives of many people, I believe it is judged. I believe it is a moral and economic failure. I believe it is bankrupt. We need to face all godless philosophies as defeated. I remember a time when I was afraid of Marxism. I made other people afraid of it, too. In time, however, as I saw into it and saw God's hand in the world, I could see it as a "rod of correction" to Christianity, but without inherent lasting success.

Secular humanism is also bankrupt. There is guilt and condemnation inside of it, and one day God will expose it. People will see that secularism is without moral foundation and will therefore produce social chaos. We don't need to be paranoid. We need to deal with it forthrightly as a defeated enemy. Secularism's walls will come down.

If we can realistically confront what we are dealing with, then we can deal with it more effectively, without ignoring it, or becoming preoccupied and fearful of it.

Seek Out Those Who Are Ready to Surrender

Finally, a major objective in knowing the enemy is to seek out those who are ready to come over to the Lord's side.

Many times those who know the enemy's system best are most ready to respond to the truth. Rahab knew the system. Joshua 2, verse 3 says, "And the king of Jericho sent word to

Rahab." The king knew, or at least knew about, this woman. She was no minor person. She was known; she had connections. Beginning with verse 8 we see what kind of intelligence her connections provided—intelligence she was able to pass on to the spies.

> Now before they lay down, she came up to them on the roof, and said to the men, "I know that the Lord has given you the land, and that the terror of you has fallen on us, and that all the inhabitants of the land have melted away before you. For we have heard how the Lord dried up the water of the Red Sea before when you came out of Egypt, and what you did to the two kings of the Amorites who were beyond the Jordan, to Sihon and Og, whom you utterly destroyed. And when we heard it, our hearts melted and no courage remained in any man any longer because of you [*This is a good look behind enemy lines.*]; for the Lord your God, He is God in heaven above and on earth beneath. [*That's good theology.*] Now therefore, please swear to me by the Lord, since I have dealt kindly with you, that you also will deal kindly with my father's household, and give me a pledge of truth. . . . (Jos 2:8-12)

These two spies had gone out in faith. There was no sign on the outside of Rahab's house saying, "House of Information." No, the spies went out not knowing where they were going, and they weren't prejudiced about whom God might use to help them.

Fear Leads to Prejudice

Sometimes God has to bring our fears to light in order to break up our prejudice.

A number of years ago, God began to do just that in my life. It was during the early days of the Jesus Movement. A young man from our church went down to a local drive-in and invited some of the kids there to come to a fellowship at the church. One of them said, "Can we bring the group?"

"Sure, bring the whole group."

Well, he didn't know that the *group* was a hard rock band. So the congregation of youth showed up at the fellowship hall for the meeting that night, and the band was already there—sun glasses and all, tuning up their instruments. They had enough mikes and PA systems to give a concert in a stadium, and they were all set up in our fellowship hall. The youth leader, in his kindness and naiveté, even allowed them to play a song. One of the girls in the youth group went outside and threw up.

Somehow we got through the evening with these kids, with them feeling that we really loved them. The drummer got converted. They began bringing their friends to our services, and pretty soon the church was full of young people who needed Christ. Finally, one Sunday morning a guru came down the aisle—medallion, robe, and everything.

We developed a reputation for being able to help street people, and one day a medical doctor came to me and said, "I have a relative who's on drugs; I've done everything medically possible for him. Can you help?" Soon I went to the young man's house. It was an old, three story house that was in need of repair. I went up the long stairs and followed a long hall to the back of the house. It was terrible; you could feel the oppression in the place. It was dark, and when I entered the room I saw the shriveled up addict, trembling in the bed. There were holes in the wall where he shot roaches with a .38 pistol.

I was supposed to tell this man about Jesus Christ!

A few days later at a subsequent visit he said, "There's someone else you need to talk to."

He took me across town to another run-down house—a terrible looking place. A fellow drew back a little slot in the door, and the next thing I knew, I was in the house and the door was quickly closed. The lights were down, and I soon realized that I was in a house of prostitution on my way to witness to a hooker. I nervously sat in the parlor while the man who brought me ran up the stairs and disappeared.

I didn't know what to do, so I started for the door. But before I could get out, the man who brought me came downstairs with his girlfriend. She had been supplying him with money for his habit. And he said, "Tell her."

"Tell her what?" I said.

"Tell her what you've been telling me."

"Here? Let's get her to church. Let's at least get out of here."

"No. You tell her right now. We don't have long."

So I told her. It seemed as though nothing happened that night. But later they both gave their hearts to the Lord, and fifteen years later I met the woman again. She said, "I just want you to know that I am still walking with God. I have a prison ministry, and every day girls are giving their hearts to Jesus Christ."

If I had had the time to think about all of this, I would have been so frightened about potential repercussions from church people that I would have been too prejudiced to probe the enemy lines. But a beautiful thing about Jesus is that, "He will not judge by what His eyes see, nor make a decision by what His ears hear" (Is 11:3). Jesus doesn't judge by appearances.

If we could see behind the walls, the people who know the system best are often the ones who are the most open to hear about Christ. That's because they understand. I don't believe anybody else in town better understood the corruption and failure of Jericho's system than Rahab did. She probably knew more leaders in that city than anybody else, and she probably knew more of what was going on, but she had come to faith in God and his purposes.

God Is Not Willing for Any to Perish

When God begins to show us the evil of a system, our predisposition is to judge it ourselves. We tend to judge everybody within that system, when God, in fact, may intend to deliver many people out of the system. We have a predisposition to condemnation. But we have to deal with this if we are to be effective for God.

Some of us have prophesied judgment so often that we will be disappointed if it doesn't happen. We've prophesied doom so often that if God doesn't doom a lot of folks, we will look like false prophets. Christians and their leaders need to repent of hostile attitudes toward the very people Christ wants to save. Let God do the judging, and let's do the preaching about his saving grace. God will judge wickedness, there's no doubt about that. But he's given *us* a redemptive purpose in the earth. God wants to use us to be the light of the world and a city set on a hill. God wants to use *you* to touch people you couldn't have touched before because you were prejudiced and hardhearted toward them. God wants to unlock his grace on you.

With such renewed minds we can face Jericho and look behind enemy lines to see the citadel for what it is. We can respect the enemy's strengths without fear and exploit his weaknesses without being presumptuous.

We need to avoid naiveté, presumption, and fear. Those are three things we don't want to have when we go into battle. God wants us to be both courageous *and* informed.

SIX

Know God's Purpose

WE BEGIN WITH COURAGE, but courage is not enough. We need intelligence, information about the enemy. But even that is not enough; we also need understanding of God's purposes.

Lately, I've been convinced that I haven't equipped people as much as I should have. I have spent too much time telling them *what* they ought to do, and not enough on *why* and *how*. The "why" and "how" probe God's purposes and methods. "Why" has to do with a deeper understanding. "How" has to do with better equipment.

God's purpose as portrayed in the story of the conquest of Jericho can be summarized in five points: (1) *to stay* with the plan, (2) *to work* through covenant, (3) *to use* God's chosen instrument, (4) *to wait* for God's timing, and (5) *to know* the victory has already been won.

1. Stay with the Plan

Joshua was well trained. He was prepared for his particular hour. He'd been under Moses' tutelage for forty years, and forty years earlier (in Numbers 13) he had been appointed to be a spy. He and eleven other men had been given the assignment of spending forty days in the land of Canaan. They had been given some specific instructions.

Don't try to do God's job. They were told to spy out the land to see what kind of a land it was. They were told to look at the people and see what kind of people were there—whether they were weak or strong, few or many. They were also told to see if the cities were fortified, if they were walled cities, and what kind of trees and fruit were in the land. The spies came back bearing a large bunch of grapes on a pole—which today is the national symbol of modern Israel.

Well, they did their job. They reported on all those things. But the problem was that they tried to do something they weren't asked to do. They tried to make a decision about *whether* they were supposed to take the land or not, and that was not what they had been sent to do. They had been sent just to get information.

God has *not* sent us out to decide whether we are supposed to take the world or not. That's his business. He has sent us out to find out *how* to take the world and to discover what kind of a world we are dealing with.

Don't pick fights. When I was first baptized in the Holy Spirit, I had very little understanding about the dynamics of the Holy Spirit. I had been raised to be careful and conservative, and I brought that with me. But I had a prayer partner whose main gift certainly wasn't caution. He was like an automobile with a big engine and no brakes, and he got me into a lot of trouble.

Our church was becoming charismatic, and his wasn't. He became very interested in demons and deliverance; he was a lot more interested in them than I was because I had enough trouble already. Anyway, he went looking for various people to deliver, and when he found some real cases he brought them to our church.

One night he brought a fellow like this to one of our meetings, and afterwards I had to take the speaker home. When

I came back to the church, the lights were low, and everyone had gone home except a few brothers. They were sharing with this fellow, and he suddenly began going over the back of a pew growling like a dog. The brothers were astounded and didn't know what to do. I was supposed to be the leader, the man with the answers, so they asked me, "What's going on?"

"That's a good question," I said, as I went over and sat down in the corner to pray. "You have to help me, Lord," I said, "because I'm the pastor here, and I don't know what's going on."

Of course, the Lord loves to teach in practical situations. So he said to me, "The power to cast out demons is like the mailman delivering the mail. If a bad dog comes after him when he is delivering the mail, he'll hit him with a stick. However, when some people find out that they can hit the dog with the stick, they throw away the mailbag and go looking for all the bad dogs in town. I'd advise you not to do that."

Sometimes we underestimate the enemy, and we go after the enemy as though *that* was our assignment. It is possible to zealously pursue something "spiritual" other than the will of God. What's important to understand is that we are supposed to disciple nations and reveal the glory of God throughout the earth. If the devil gets in our way, hit him with the stick. And you will need the stick. Use everything God's given us, but remember: our purpose is to deliver the message and take the land. I believe the Lord wants to give us the earth. "The meek shall inherit the earth." "The earth is the Lord's and the fullness thereof." "The glory of God will cover the earth." It's God's purpose for us to stay with his plan and purpose for us.

2. Work through Covenant

Let's again consider what happened in Jericho. The Holy Spirit had led the two spies to a harlot's house. She gave them all the vital information they needed to inspire the Israelites for their fight. Then she saved their lives by deflecting the authorities when they came searching for the men. She had already done a lot for them.

But Rahab was no fool.

Not only was she wise enough to believe that God would help the Israelites win, she also knew she was doomed unless she could work a deal. The two spies were still trapped in a locked, walled city with the king's men looking for them, so Rahab said:

"Now therefore, please swear to me by the Lord, since I have dealt kindly with you, that you also will deal kindly with my father's household, and give me a pledge of truth, and spare my father and my mother and my brothers and my sisters, with all who belong to them, and deliver our lives from death." So the men said to her, "Our life for yours if you do not tell this business of ours; and it shall come to pass about when the Lord gives us the land that we will deal kindly and faithfully with you." Then she let them down by a rope through the window, for her house was on the city wall, so that she was living on the wall. And she said to them, "Go to the hill country, lest the pursuers happen upon you, and hide yourselves there for three days, until the pursuers return. Then afterward you may go on your way." And the men said to her, "We shall be free from this oath to you which you have made us swear, unless, when we come into the land, you tie this cord of scarlet thread in the window through which you let us down. . . ." And she said, "According to your words, so be it." So she sent them away, and they departed; and she tied the scarlet cord in the window. (Jos 2:12-18, 21)

This woman used strategy, and we need a more strategic mentality for our warfare. We don't need to just stand around and lob our bombs; we need strategy.

The Establishment of Covenant. Rahab made a *covenant* with the spies and they with her. God deals from a covenant basis.

The final card up Rahab's sleeve was her offer of safe passage in exchange for her life, and the spies agreed.

They made a covenant with this woman because of her confession of faith in the purposes of God. Even though she had been immoral and idolatrous, she had a heart for God, and they saw it. They spiritually discerned her heart and dealt with her on a spiritual, not a carnal, basis, and she became leverage for God in the city of Jericho.

Not only that, but she was selected for the lineage of Jesus. In that very moment when she was faithful to what the Holy Spirit of God was saying to her, she was selected for the lineage of our Lord. In the Gospels there are only four women (besides Mary, the mother of Jesus) who are mentioned in Christ's lineage and they are: Tamar, Rahab, Ruth, and Bathsheba. Tamar tricked her father-in-law, Jacob, into sleeping with her. Rahab was a harlot. Ruth was a Moabitess. And Bathsheba was an adultress. But in all four cases, God redeemed them.

Let's not preclude what God will do. God will get folks out of the citadel of sin. He will get people out of the Jerichos of this world, and if we'll use our spiritual discernment instead of our carnal judgment, God can pull the walls down.

Don't say that God can't pull down "the walls" in your town to his glory and build his city in its place. Don't say that he can't move into Washington D.C. and turn it upside down for his glory. Don't prejudge what God can do. God can do all things (through us) if we'll believe in him.

Mutual Confidence. There is another example of covenant represented in this story. Joshua had a lot of confidence in these two men, and they had a lot of confidence in Joshua. It was a covenant relationship. There was a bond between them.

They didn't shrink from telling their report. These brothers faced their debriefing with ease because they had confidence in their relationship with Joshua. It was a covenant relationship. They were open and trusting. They trusted their leader. He trusted them. There wasn't any debate about the unusualness of the way God works.

We need to develop covenant relationships. If we are to work strategically, we will *have* to trust each other in covenant relationships because we all have different jobs. We have to trust that the other man is doing his job. When a man comes back and says that this is what God did, we won't put him through the third degree.

It's God's purpose for us to work through covenant.

3. Use God's Chosen Instrument

I suspect that most of us would have a difficult time if a harlot was to be the instrument of God, and we knew about it in advance. We sing about the Word, but when we try to live what it talks about, it gets interesting. And this story does.

Scripture says, "And such were some of you," in First Corinthians 6:11, meaning some of them had been gross sinners. It's easy for us to forget that we were all sinners. But sometimes those of us who have been at the very center of the enemy's camp are the ones most ready to respond to God's guiding. We can't afford to reject anyone whom the Lord may want to use as our ally.

When I was first baptized in the Holy Spirit, I was scared. I thought that I would be fired from my church because almost every Baptist preacher I knew who experienced the baptism of the Holy Spirit with accompanying signs got fired; if he didn't get fired, he was so strongly urged to leave that he did before there was a chance to fire him.

It was Christmas time, my wife and I had a six-month-old baby, and we didn't have much money. We had just moved into a house, and we had almost no furniture. We were very young (I was about 27 years old), and I thought I was going to lose my pastorate. It was a lonely and dark time for me.

Then I got a phone call from a woman who said, "You don't know me, but I want to do something for you."

Immediately my attention was arrested and I said, "What is it?"

"I want to buy you some furniture."

"Well, who are you?" I asked.

"It's none of your business. I just want to do this for you."

I said, "Now, wait a minute; I need to know who you are."

"No you don't," she answered.

"But I don't know what your motives are."

She said, "I don't have any motives. I just want to do this. You're a man of God, aren't you?"

"Well, I believe I'm a man of God."

"Then I believe God spoke to me and told me to help you out."

"I appreciate it, but you understand this doesn't buy you anything with God, doesn't get you into heaven, or anything else. Do you understand that?"

She said, "Yes." I tried to witness to her, but she said, "Look, I just want you to go down to the furniture store. I know you preachers will buy something cheap, so I've told them the *minimum* dollar amount you can buy; I want you to buy furniture to total *at least* that dollar amount. Then go around the corner to the art store. They have some paintings for you. The drapery store will call you later for an appointment to measure your house for drapes."

I couldn't get over all this. Here I was in the middle of the worst conflict I could imagine in my church, I was about to be fired at Christmas time, we had a new baby, and we had no money. I thought, "My, this is an answer from God!" We rejoiced and thanked God, and I later told this story often to testify to God's goodness. One time after I told the story, a man came to me and said, "If I were you, I wouldn't give that testimony."

I said, "Why not?"

"Because I think I know who that woman is."

"You do?"

"Yeah. She runs a house of prostitution down on lower Government Street," and he began to describe her to me. "So you see," he said, "I wouldn't tell anybody about that."

I thought, *Isn't that something!* The Lord wanted to bless me, but he had to pass up all the preachers, all the churches, and go through all of the city until he finally found someone to help me out, and that willing person who heard from God was a prostitute. This helped me to identify with the story of Rahab. I'm not advocating immoral practices; I'm simply saying, don't *you* determine who God can use and who he can't. Don't try to guess in advance what God might do or what he might not do because he'll fool you every time. It's his purpose and he can choose the instruments whoever they may be.

4. *Wait for God's Timing*

God is a God of ironies. Just when we think we have God figured out, he does something we never expected. And often it is in the matter of timing:

> And they [the spies] departed and came to the hill country, and *remained there for three days* until the pursuers returned. Now the pursuers had sought them all along the road, but had not found them. Then the two men returned and came down from the hill country and crossed over and came to Joshua the son of Nun, and they related to him all that had happened to them. And they said to Joshua, "Surely the Lord has given all the land into our hands, and all the inhabitants of the land, moreover, have melted away before us." (Jos 2:22-24)

I'm sure the two spies from Jericho could hardly wait to get home with their good news. Furthermore, the longer they stayed in hostile territory, the greater were their chances of getting captured. They wanted to return immediately to Joshua, but that wasn't God's plan. It wasn't his time for them to go home, and I'm sure they wondered why.

Some of us also wrestle with not having a quick escape. Sometimes it is from our immediate situation, but sometimes it is the big Escape we want. The Scriptures acknowledge that we "groan within ourselves, waiting eagerly for" our freedom and coming glory. That's normal, but we need to trust God's timing. We need to accept why God is waiting: he's not willing that any should perish. We need to see the whole world as part of the promise to be obtained.

There is a mystery that's at work here, and a mystery is something we can't understand. The Kingdom of God is a mystery. Sometimes we want to have it all spelled out, so we try to figure out every detail of God's future plans and his timing. Our basic problem is the tendency to want to be God instead of trusting God.

I remember when I had the entire future on Bible prophecy charts. I've seen charts stretched all the way across the front of the church. The only reason we didn't have more prophecy is because we did not have wider buildings. I preached an entire year out of Revelation, six months out of Daniel, and three months out of Ezekiel. I know about that approach.

I don't want to make fun of anybody who thinks he understands it all, but you will miss the Holy Spirit unless you open your heart both to God's ultimate purpose and his timing. I'm not talking about any theological position—pre-, post-, or mid-tribulation. I'm talking about accepting God's timing and following Jesus Christ in these crucial days by letting *him* unlock history for us and bring us to our destiny in him.

Theological presuppositions won't hinder God, but they may keep us from hearing and following God. They may cause us to become discouraged due to misinterpretations of events. You may be discouraged because you've been attacking spiritual forces, but you have not seen the victory yet. Don't throw away your confidence. Wait on God's timing.

5. *Know the Victory Has Already Been Won*

I like the way Joshua 2 concludes: "And they [the spies] said to Joshua, 'Surely the Lord has given all the land into our hands, and all the inhabitants of the land, moreover, have melted away before us.'"

They returned with their mission accomplished. All they did

was what the Holy Spirit led them to do. That's all. When they got through with their business, they went home and told Joshua everything.

Did they say, "The Lord *might* give us the land" or "The Lord *is going* to give us the land?" No. They said: "The Lord *has* given us the land!" That means it had already been done. Victory was based on the presupposition that it was already finished. The people didn't go into the land trying to win it. They went into the land knowing that they had won it. And, likewise, we can't win unless we believe God has already won the victory.

That's a good feeling, and it makes all the difference in the world! What I'm saying is very simple: There is a tremendous difference between trying to win and believing I've already won. It is the difference between striving and resting. It is the difference between anxiety and peace. It is the difference between misery and joy.

Consider the Israelites. They hadn't even crossed the river yet. They hadn't done anything. All they had was the report from a couple of spies who said, "It's already done." But the Israelites believed that God had already given it to them.

As a boy I had a best friend; we grew up together, went to all twelve years of school together, and played sports together. In our senior year, we played a championship football game with another school across the county. Their team was bigger than we were; they were better than we were. But my friend and I were covenant buddies. We were selected co-captains that night, and as we walked out on the field before the game, I looked at him and he looked at me, and I said, "It's in the bag!"

He said, "We can't miss. It's just a matter of time."

Well, it was quite a game. The opposing team was older and bigger and favored to win. The boy who played against me outweighed me by a hundred pounds. But I knew in my heart that the other team was finished. Even when they were on our eight yard line just before the game was over, I still knew the game was ours. Even though I got knocked "colder than a fish," I had no doubts. When I came to, everything was flashing and screaming. The coach had me carried off the field and asked me, "Do you know the score?" Like a fool I told him, so he put me back in.

The other team had been running up and down the field at will, but they just hadn't scored. Every time they got close, they fumbled, or something would go wrong. And then when they were down on our eight yard line with a couple of minutes left, we called time out. I went around to all the fellows and said, "This is it! This is it!" Everybody got pumped up, and when we got back in the line, I told that fellow who outweighed me by a hundred pounds, "You might as well move, because we're coming through."

And we did. They lost five yards on the next play and five yards on the next play, and before we knew it, the game was over. We won because we believed that we had already won.

If one can believe that kind of thing about a football game, and if we believe that Jesus Christ died and rose again and gave us a blood covenant, how much more should we believe that the land is already ours!

We need to put more emphasis on what happened in the first coming of Christ. Many people don't believe that Jesus finished the task he came to do. They think he has to come back to do it. Don't misunderstand me; I believe in the reality of the second coming of Jesus Christ. But I want you to understand something that's *going* to happen. He already is seated. When he died on the cross, he said, "It *is* finished." He has won the victory; we're his Body, the land is ours.

Some of us act as though he didn't rise from the dead. Some of us act as though he didn't ascend to the Father's right hand. Some of us act as though all authority and power haven't been given to him.

Let's not say, "By the grace of God we might win." We need to say, "The battle is won! The land is ours!" It's just a matter of how we will be led to do the will of God and how he will give it to us. That makes all the difference in the world.

We have a challenge to face our Jerichos. There's a citadel in front of you, and the walls are just as high and just as thick as those that the Israelites faced. The enemy is hiding behind them, and he is defying you. But the promises of God are awaiting you, and they must be obtained.

Israel's presupposition was possession, and your presupposition must be possession, too. I'm not suggesting presumption. If you don't know the will of God, then you'd better find it out. But if God has promised that what is before you is yours, and he died for you to have it, and he has told you that you are more than a conqueror through Jesus Christ, then I suggest that you don't try to find some other way to enter the land. Go ahead in the victory that Christ has already won. Act on it.

SEVEN

Commit Yourself to Victory

A LL OF US NEED TO KNOW what our calling is. Joshua could never have been Moses, Moses could never have been Abraham, and Abraham could never have been David. Each person is unique. Each one of us needs to know our call and what God wants us to do.

Joshua's call was to bring deliverance—remember, his name meant, "God's salvation." So his call was to bring deliverance to the people of Israel by bringing them into the land, delivering the land out of the hands of the enemy, and leading the people to obtain God's promises.

The Book of Joshua is a military book, a book about strategy and conquest. Sometimes we read the Bible symbolically when, in fact, what's recorded there happened in reality. We tend to "spiritualize" the Scriptures, more than we should.

Joshua was not your typical clergyman. He was a warrior-leader. Like Joshua, we need to be militant about our objectives. Our weapons are not carnal, *but they are mighty through God, able to pull down strongholds.* Remember: "We wrestle not against flesh and blood," *but we do wrestle!* We need to come to grips with that reality.

The River Jordan is a type of death. It stands between the

wanderings in the wilderness and a new life on the other side. To pass through the Jordan, the people must have a commitment to follow the Presence of God into doing the will of God. It means crossing the point of no return. This commitment gets rather serious, but it has to be there if we're going to win.

Coming to the Place of Commitment

Let's take a lesson from Joshua. In any serious contest, there comes a moment when we have to be committed to the contest for better or worse, win or lose. What does it mean to come to this place of commitment—commitment to the task, commitment to each other?

Win or Die. As a church we got into a real battle with the IRS a number of years ago. It was a five-year audit which took three and a half years to accomplish. The IRS zeroed in on us, and we didn't know why. We found out later that someone had stolen records out of our files, made false accusations based on these records taken out of context, and forwarded it to the IRS; but, of course, we didn't know that at the time, so we had no idea why the IRS focused on us. But we found ourselves in a life-and-death battle for our survival as a church.

Our first impression was, "The government is our friend" (and I believe it usually is), so when we got the letters saying we would be audited, we took the posture that we would cooperate in all things. We hired a *friendly* Spirit-filled lawyer and sent the IRS whatever they wanted.

But after we spent $12,000 on attorney's fees, answering questions which didn't satisfy them, and after getting the runaround when we questioned why we were being audited, we decided to change our strategy. We released our *friendly* Christian lawyer, and we hired an *aggressive* Christian lawyer. We decided that we were dealing with an enemy in the IRS. We sued the government on the Freedom of Information Act, and we discovered my files in their files. It's illegal to steal, even if it's the government that does it, so that scuttled their case even though their case was not a case. It was only after spending over $100,000 on five different attorneys and the bureaucratic process that we learned our lessons.

If we do the will of God, we will have our wars. There will come a time and place in the battle when it boils down to a "win or die" commitment. In this instance, we had some bad publicity, which some people—and the government—believed. There were some Christian brothers who had strong feelings against us and who fueled this investigation against us.

In the middle of this battle with the IRS, the elders of our church didn't know what would happen. We didn't know if it would cost us our homes, our tax status, or our influence with the church. We could lose everything and everybody! So we got together in a room and committed ourselves to win or die. We joined our hands together and said, "This attack is not of God, this is of the devil. We have responsibilities as shepherds and pastors, and we are hereby in the presence of God going to make a solemn commitment to see this thing through. We join our hearts together that God in his righteousness will vindicate us because we know we've done nothing wrong."

Well, God in his mercy did vindicate us. After our experience, we helped change the law of the land. We initiated the Church Audit Procedures Act, which passed through Congress. We helped change the IRS code so that when they ever do that again, they'll have to pay up to $25,000 in attorneys' fees for the people they do it to. God helped us not to be bitter and unforgiving, and we used our experience, plus all the money it cost us, as "tuition" for a higher degree in God.

At least die on your terms. You never know where your enemy's stronghold is, or what weapon he'll use. Something out there may be fighting your church, or trying to destroy your family. But to win the battle, you must begin by making a commitment. You can't win a war if you're not committed. If you don't intend to win, get out of the danger zone! But if you intend to win, commit yourself to it.

However, you need to know that all commitments are in faith. Nobody ever knows how it will work out. You do it in trust to God. You don't commit yourself to people because you trust human beings. You are going to have your feelings hurt, anyway, but don't worry. You're not merely trusting in people, you're trusting God. You're doing it because God said to do it. Everything—including our relationships—is under God.

When we joined our hands together in that spiritual war for our church, it was not because we trusted each other 100 percent. We were only men and could have failed each other. But we made the commitment because we had reached the point where we had to. We did it as unto God, and God is faithful. When men let you down, God doesn't let you down. Every commitment is for better or for worse. The preacher says, "Do you commit yourself to this woman or this man for better or for worse?" Sometimes it gets worse! "Rich or poor?" Sometimes you get poor! You have to know that the alternative does exist. But you need to be ready to make a commitment.

Jesus said to the church in Laodicea, "You're lukewarm, you're not hot or cold; you nauseate me" (Rv 3:15, 16, paraphrased). God would rather deal with us in our coldness than in our being lukewarm. If we hold back because of the danger, we'll never know the victories.

We have to understand something else about the Israelites. They had wandered for forty years. They knew what it was like *not* to make a commitment. They knew what it was to come up against the problem and run from it, and they didn't want any more of it. They had come to the place where they would rather die fighting than die wandering.

If you're going to die anyway, why not die for the right reason? If you give up your life, give it for something worthwhile. Die on your terms and not the enemy's terms!

Commit Yourself to the Basics of Spiritual Victory

We cannot proceed until we are willing to commit ourselves to the basic necessities of spiritual victory. We cannot lead our people without basic commitment, for to do so is to lead them into certain trouble. We can't lead them beyond their willingness to be committed to the purposes of God.

Before the Israelites could proceed into the land, they had to commit themselves to a number of basics:

Commit yourself to God's purpose. The people of Israel committed themselves to a future of deliverance—finally. They knew from experience what happened when they lost sight of the vision God had laid out for their future.

We need to commit ourselves to the future. Some Christians are trying to escape the future, but as *Futurist Magazine* (March, 1979), said, "One of the basic necessities of life is a vision of the future in which one has enough faith to act."

When we say "basic necessity," we're talking about things like food, clothing, and shelter. A vision for the future is also a *basic necessity*. When we lose our vision and hope for the future, we lose our confidence to act. We become wanderers; our lives become debilitating. We need to put before our people a vision of the future that they can commit themselves to act on with great hope and expectation. That's part of the basic necessity of leadership.

In 1917 the communists were marching around Red Square in Russia shouting, "We'll change the world! We'll change the world! We'll change the world!" The Christians about that time started saying, "We'll get out of the world! We'll get out of the world! We'll get out of the world!" The communists have changed the world, but God hasn't taken us out of it. I believe the Christians should begin saying, "We'll change the world! We'll change the world!"

Jesus told us to change the world. As long as we're here, we are to be his light in the world, the salt of the earth, the army of God.

Commit yourself to leaders. The Israelites committed themselves to Joshua.

> And they answered Joshua saying, "All that you have commanded us we will do, and wherever you send us we will go. Just as we obeyed Moses in all things, so we will obey you. Only may the Lord your God be with you, as He was with Moses." (Jos 1:16-17)

It's biblical to make commitments to leaders. We need to know what kind of commitment we're making, and what for, but woe be to the leader who's trying to lead uncommitted constituents.

They said, "Joshua, all that you command us we will do." They couldn't have made it any plainer than that. That's a pretty tough commitment. We see this kind of commitment in the New Testament as well. The apostle Paul made certain commandments regarding followers in the epistles. A commitment to leaders is basic if we're going to do the will of God.

Some churches are defeated because they have no commitment to direction, no commitment to leadership. The leader can't make a decisive move in a moment of necessity because he knows he doesn't have the backing of his people.

Have you ever seen an army that was run like a democracy? If you get on a ship, even a civilian ship, democracy is over with. Ships have captains, not chairmen. I'm not against democracy, but in a military situation, you have to understand you're in a military mode; there has to be strong leadership, and there has to be commitment to that leadership, or you're done for in the middle of the fray.

Commit yourself to each other. Any group of people that wishes to constitute themselves into a nation first forms a covenant, and they commit themselves to it. We don't have to make a new covenant; one has already been made for all who place themselves under the blood of Jesus Christ. But we have to commit ourselves to it. We must realize that if we accept the covenant of Jesus Christ, we accept everybody that Jesus Christ has accepted because his covenant binds us all together. We don't always act like it, but it's a fact.

The problem is, we're just like the twelve tribes of Israel were. We are divided into numerous branches of Christendom, and then we're divided into various denominational and nondenominational tribes, and even our denominations are divided, using all sorts of qualifying titles in their names. We love to divide ourselves.

But we have to remember, God delivered *all* the people out of Egypt, and he wanted to bring them *all* into the Land of Promise. Even the two and a half tribes that wanted to claim their inheritance on the east side of the River Jordan went *with their brothers* to obtain the promises of God *for their brothers*.

We can't afford to stop short with a vision of the future that is just for our church. God's promises are for all those who call him Lord. When we are committed to the purposes of God, we can commit ourselves *to* each other *for* each other.

Covenant is a bond that differentiates God's people from the noncovenant people of the world. It's the basis for government. It's the foundation for action.

When we commit ourselves to the purposes of God for the future, to our leaders, and to one another, we commit ourselves to the basic necessities for spiritual victory. Then the Spirit of God will begin to move.

EIGHT

Following the Presence of God

J OSHUA 1 IS ABOUT *courage*—the courage to commit to the task. Joshua 2 is about *information*—getting the information we need to do the task. Joshua 3 is about *following the Presence of God* through death into purpose.

The River Jordan is a type of death. It stands between the wanderings in the wilderness and a new life on the other side. To pass through the Jordan, the people had to commit themselves to follow the Presence of God into a commitment to the will of God. It means crossing the point of no return. This commitment got rather serious, but it had to exist if they were going to win.

And it came about at the end of three days that the officers went through the midst of the camp; and they commanded the people, saying "When you see the ark of the covenant of the Lord your God with the Levitical priests carrying it, then you shall set out from your place and go after it. However, there shall be between you and it a distance of about 2,000 cubits by measure. Do not come near it, that you may know the way by which you shall go, for you have not passed this way before." Then Joshua said to the people, "Consecrate yourselves, for tomorrow the Lord will do wonders among you." And Joshua spoke to the priests, saying, "Take up the ark of the covenant and cross over ahead of the people." So they took up the ark of the covenant and went ahead of the people. (Jos 3:2-6)

Finding the Point of Reference

Commitment is not an end in itself. To make progress, we have to find our point of reference. What is it that, when it moves, we're going to follow? I believe the point of reference for progress in the church is the Presence of God.

God's Presence: Our focal point. Every purpose has a focal point. Every person needs a focal point. For Noah it was an ark. For Abraham it was a city and a son. For Jesus it was the cross. If he had not gone to the cross he would have missed the Presence because the Presence was leading him inextricably to the cross. For every leader and group of people there's a focal point where the Presence of God will lead them to fulfill their eternal purpose.

I don't always love the will of God, but I love the Presence. When the will and Presence of God is going one way, and I start going another way . . . I miss the Presence. That's what brings me back to the will of God. I would rather suffer in the will of God and have the Presence than be without the Presence.

When the Israelites sinned against God by making the golden calf, God lifted his Presence. Moses took the tabernacle down, and pitched it a good distance from the camp; if anyone sought the Lord he had to go outside the camp (Ex 33). The Presence left! Then Moses had a dialogue with God, one of the most beautiful passages in the Bible. God said, "Go on up to the land I promised you. I'll send an angel and drive out your enemies. But my Presence won't go with you" (see Ex 33:1-3).

You can get a lot of things without the Presence of God. You can claim the promises; you can force it sometimes. God said, "OK, Go ahead; I'll send the angel, and I'll give you the land." But then Moses said: *"If your Presence doesn't go with us, I don't want to go"* (see Ex 33:15). He wasn't after what God could give him; he was after God! So God decided to go up with him.

The Presence of God is what leads us to the will of God and the purpose of God.

The ark of the covenant: Christ in the midst of the people. For the Israelites, the focal point of God's Presence was the ark. It was a very small box, only three and three-quarter feet long, two and one quarter feet wide, and two and one quarter feet high, made of wood overlaid with gold. In it was Aaron's rod that budded, the two tables of stone on which the law was written, and a potful of manna. The lid of the ark formed a "mercy seat" over which two golden cherubim peered with outspread wings. This ark was a type of Christ. It represented the "bread of life" (the manna), the authority of his priesthood and life triumphing over death (the rod), God's Word (the law), his humanity overlaid with his deity (the wood overlaid with gold).

The ark was the most holy thing that Israel had. It was called the ark of the covenant because it was the symbol of God's bond with his people, a foretaste of Christ, our bond with God the Father. It was the place where the atoning blood was sprinkled, where the mercy of God was given, the place of redemption which the cherubs peered down on in great mystery; it was the physical token of his faithfulness and Presence.

The people followed the ark. When the cloud of the Presence of God moved, the ark moved, and when the ark moved, the people moved. When they were camped out in the wilderness, the ark was right in the middle—three tribes camped on the east side, three on the south side, three on the west side, and three on the north side. They stayed there as long as the cloud was over the ark. But when the cloud—the Presence—started to move, the Levites took the ark and started moving. Then the people started moving, and the ark became their focal point of following the Presence of God.

Following the Presence. I believe the Presence of God is still the thing we have to follow because the Presence will lead us to our purpose, and our purpose may lead us to war. Woe be to the man who loves war so much that he goes looking for trouble and doesn't follow the Presence, because he will be defeated. The Presence is our point of reference. We need to follow the Presence into the purpose of God; when the Presence leads us into battle, our lives may be on the line, but God's purpose will prevail.

Before I was converted in 1951, I wrestled with the Presence of God. I wanted to be a Christian, but I didn't believe I *could* be a Christian. I was a member of a church, but I wasn't a Christian so I wrestled with the convicting presence of the Holy Spirit. Finally I trusted Christ to make me a Christian.

In 1955, when God called me to be a preacher, I didn't want to be a preacher, but I wanted the Presence of God; I wanted the blessing of God. I went through that agony of losing the Presence, and finally I surrendered to the call because I wanted his Presence.

In 1963, when I was spiritually dry, I didn't want to be a Pentecostal. I didn't want to speak in tongues. Tongues seemed like nothing but trouble to me. I wasn't looking for tongues, I was looking for the Presence! But the Presence moved me right into a pentecostal experience. I spoke in tongues, and many other things happened that I wasn't looking for. But I was following the Presence.

It's a difficult thing when the Presence starts going somewhere you don't want to go. I wanted the Presence to move up the denominational ladder, or to move into certain circles that were appealing to me. But the Presence wasn't moving me that way. It was moving me to a new place, against all my roots, history, heritage, ambition. Everything in me said, "Go that way," and the Presence said, "Go this way."

You have to follow the Presence because the Presence has a purpose that's different than yours. If you're following your understanding and your logic, you're missing the focal point, the Presence of God.

God's ark is borne by anointed men. The ark was borne on the shoulders of appointed and anointed men, not on "cattle carts" of human engineering. God anoints people.

When the Philistines captured and then returned the ark, how did they move it? On a cattle cart (1 Sm 6). The first time David moved the ark, what did he do? He had it set on a cattle cart the cart nearly upset, and Uzzah died trying to steady the ark (2 Sm 6). We need to see that the tokens of God's covenant are carried by God's anointed.

God anoints people, and if we reject God's anointed servants, we'll have problems with the God who anoints them. We have to take the people, too. God has a problem with people who want a gift but don't want the person God uses to bring it to them. We need to receive one another, not just each other's gifts.

Bob Mumford talks about "coke bottle relationships," in which you just turn the person up, take the contents, and then throw the person away. There are many men and women of God who have been thrown away after people used them up. We need to embrace the instrument God appoints, not just the anointing.

Keep Your Perspective

". . . there shall be between you and it [the ark] a distance of about 2,000 cubits by measure. Do not come near it, that you may know the way by which you shall go, for you have not passed this way before." (Jos 3:4)

God said, "When the ark starts to move, don't get too close to it. Stay about three-fifths of a mile behind it." In their awe of

God they walked very slowly. That could have put them as much as twenty minutes behind the ark.

God said, "When that ark starts to move, don't get too close to it. Keep your perspective—because you've never passed this way before." Over familiarity indicates pride and that we think we know where we're going. Forty years had taught them to follow with care. When we realize we don't know where we're going, we will follow at a respectful distance, observe the Holy Spirit, and not be overly familiar with the things of God.

One of the great dangers in coming into the things of God is to get too familiar with God and try to demystify what he is doing. The pride of knowledge will cause us to stumble and hurt ourselves. It may cause us to "touch the ark" when we shouldn't. Familiarity can hurt us.

We need to maintain a sense of awe and mystery at all times with the things of God. Sometimes I see people who were raised in the things of the Spirit lose their respect for those things. Other people have come to appreciate those same things at great price. Let me encourage you: If you have been around the mysteries of the Spirit a long time, don't ever cease to be amazed at what God does, and don't ever cease to realize that he can do more than you've seen him do.

Our society can't stand a mystery. Humanistic and egalitarian philosophies have affected even the church; we have to "understand" everything and pull it down to our level. It's what one fellow called "crabology." An old man was fishing for crabs on the end of a pier. He let the wire basket down with some meat in it, the crabs crawled into it, he pulled them up and took them out and he threw them into a bushel basket, one after another. The crabs in the bushel basket were trying to get out, climbing up the sides. A fellow came by and said, "Those crabs are going to get out of there."

"Naw," the old man said, "they won't get out," and he just kept throwing them in the basket.

And the fellow said, "Look, you have a lot of crabs in there, they're almost up on the side now."

"Naw," the old man said, "you don't know anything about crabology."

"What do you mean, crabology?"

"Well, if you knew anything about crabology, you'd know that about the time one of those crabs gets up to the edge, those other crabs are going to pull him back down."

The truth is that we get overly familiar with God and overly familiar with each other, and we don't respect the things of God or respect one another. The next thing you know we're criticizing, pulling everything down, and all progress is halted. Christians can be like crabs. Sometimes we anger God because we are being motivated by pride and arrogance to handle things that we really don't understand.

Rationalism cannot tolerate mystery. Rationalism is nothing more than a radical manifestation of human arrogance. If we say, "This is a mystery," the rationalists will say, "No, there's a logical explanation in there somewhere."

I'm glad I've learned to accept the existence of mystery. Let me say this: a mystery will work for you if you'll accept it as a mystery. If you start taking it apart and analyzing it, it loses something. By the time you get it all figured out, it has quit working. It's like a dissected frog. It's all there but it doesn't jump any more. There's something about coming to the mysteries of God, in the fear of God, that makes them powerful in your life.

Marriage is a mystery! How two people can become one is a mystery. The complementarity of the sexes is a mystery. When you lose your sense of mystery about your marriage, something goes out of it.

The church is a mystery! There's a mystery about how it operates: the call to both leadership and servanthood, to be the Body of Christ on earth, to discern sin but withhold from judging others.

The Kingdom of God is a mystery! Even Jesus didn't try to explain everything. He used parables: "The Kingdom of God is like a sower . . . a mustard seed . . . yeast in bread dough . . . a hidden treasure . . . a costly pearl." He said, "It's a mystery!" Yet some of us think we have it all figured out.

When the ark moved out of the Tabernacle, they covered it up. It was a mystery. Later in the temple the ark sat behind the veil, hidden in the Holy of Holies. Some of the mystery has been removed. The veil in the temple has been torn, and the blood of Jesus Christ allows us into the Presence of God. We can come freely into his gracious Presence. But we must never forget by what price we enter God's Presence; we must not lose our sense of awe and respect for the mysterious work of God. We must not become too familiar, arrogant, or assume we know where God is leading. For "we have not passed this way before."

Look for God's Sign of Total Victory

Then Joshua said to the people, "Consecrate yourselves, for tomorrow the Lord will do wonders among you." (Jos 3:5)

Israel had moved right to the edge of the Jordan. The commanders had passed through the camp giving the people final instructions, and then Joshua spoke to the people: "Consecrate yourselves, because some things will happen that have never happened to you before. The supernatural is going to be restored to Israel, and the things that were done in the beginning days of your fathers will be done again in your day."

I imagine a great sense of excitement came upon the people. The great signs and wonders of the exodus from Egypt were but a memory and a legend. The younger adults had been born in the wilderness and had only heard of the parting of the Red Sea. What was going to happen? What did it mean?

Exalting the leader.

Now the Lord said to Joshua, "This day I will begin to exalt you in the sight of all Israel, that they may know that just as I have been with Moses, I will be with you. You shall, moreover, command the priests who are carrying the ark of the covenant, saying 'When you come to the edge of the waters of the Jordan, you shall stand still in the Jordan.'" Then Joshua said to the sons of Israel, "Come here, and hear the words of the Lord your God." And Joshua said, "By this you shall know that the living God is among you, and that He will assuredly dispossess from before you the Canaanite, the Hittite, the Hivite, the Perizzite, the Girgashite, the Amorite, and the Jebusite." (Jos 3:7-10)

First of all God said, "I'm going to exalt you, Joshua. I will make a name for you, just like I did Moses. I'll do for you what I did for Moses."

This can be abused, so we must use caution here. We should never use authority in a self-serving manner, but I believe that God wants to raise up great leaders in our day, leaders that even the world will come to fear and respect. I think it has to happen. I don't believe that we can make much progress without strong leadership.

It's not the world that's torn church leaders down; it's the church. And it's not just the church, leaders tear down each other.

I believe there are leaders among leaders. In any group God will anoint leadership for that group because God's not an anarchist. In the Kingdom of God there are stewards over ten cities, over five cities, and so forth. God exalts leadership so that the people of God can be ruled in righteousness, peace, and joy, and also so they can be marshalled to conquer unconquered territories.

The implementation of this theory doesn't always work well. Leaders have not always waited for God to exalt them, but have exalted themselves. Some leaders have gotten so enthusiastic about *leading* God's people that they forget to *serve* God's people.

But God said to Joshua, "I'm going to exalt you, Joshua."

People sometimes tell me, "God never honors anybody." But

God said, for example, "I'm going to honor you, David," and he did. Some people say, "That will take away from God's glory and honor." God's not insecure. People who can't honor others are insecure, and they think God has the same psychological problem that they have; he doesn't. It doesn't bother God if somebody else gets honored. God himself honors people. The Bible says that God will honor all those that honor him. Don't be nervous if people get honored. Flattery is something else; that's deceitful. But honor is of God.

God said, "I'm going to do the same things for you that I did for Moses."

God has a special interest in the person who carries responsibility. God honored Moses because Moses responded to God's call. It was Moses and God on the mountain having the discussion around the burning bush; it was Moses and God when the plagues started coming; it was Moses and God when Pharaoh threatened his life. Moses stood his ground and God said, *"I like you!"*

When Moses had to face the Red Sea, God said, "I will honor you Moses. You stood by me, you did what I told you to do." God will always honor his call.

Moses obeyed God and had brought out the Israelites, surrounded by the desert and the mountains and the sea and the army, and a most vicious and hardened ruler was chasing them. As they confronted the Red Sea Moses said, "Now what are we going to do, Lord?"

God said, "Take that stick you have and stretch it out, and I'll open up the waters." Moses lifted his stick and the waters started to open up. God honored Moses. *Then* Israel honored him. "Ah," they said, "Moses is wonderful."

It's hard to lead a people after they have been led by a Moses. No matter what Joshua did, he'd hear, "Our fathers told us how it was that day when Moses stretched out his rod over the Red Sea. Moses was a great leader!" But God said, "Joshua, I'll fix that. I'm going to honor you; you'll have your own miracle. I'll show them that I can do it for you, just as I did for Moses."

Joshua said, "The ark bearers go first into the water. I don't want them shoving everybody else in; I want them to go." If you're carrying the ark, you are first in the water. He said, "God's going to do a miracle, and when this miracle happens, you'll know that the living God is in your midst."

God's sign is the supernatural. That's why God does miracles. Healings are wonderful, deliverances are wonderful, and they have their own by-products and blessings. But a real purpose of miracles is to know that God is in our midst.

Gideon was threshing wheat in a wine press to save it from the Midianites (Jgs 6); he was very frightened, but the angel of God came and said, "*O valiant warrior.*"

"Shhh, the Midianites will hear you."

But the angel continued, "The Lord is with you!"

Gideon was no fool; he said, "If God is with us, where are the miracles he did in the days of our fathers?" That's the first question. If God is in our midst, where's the supernatural?

The angel said, "You're going to know that the living God, the God of all the earth, is with you and in your midst, and the supernatural is the *token* that I'm going to drive out all of your enemies."

I believe that. When someone is healed, we shouldn't just say, "Thank God he healed brother so-and-so"; we should say, "The living God is in our midst!" Then all kinds of things can start happening. The supernatural is the sign of total victory. If God is for us, who can be against us?

God had been preparing Israel for this hour, a milestone in history. The manifest victory was still in the distance, across the Jordan, behind the walls of Jericho. But God would show his hand: the supernatural would be a sign of God's total victory. "*By this you shall know* that the living God is among you. . . .": he will defeat your enemies (see Jos 3:10).

Crossing the Point of No Return

We've come to the place of commitment, we've found our point of reference, we've seen that the supernatural is the sign of total victory, and now we're ready to cross the point of no return.

> [Joshua said:] "Behold, the ark of the covenant of the Lord of all the earth is crossing over ahead of you into the Jordan."
> ... So it came about when the people set out from their tents to cross the Jordan with the priests carrying the ark of the covenant before the people, and when those who carried the ark came into the Jordan, and the feet of the priests carrying the ark were dipped in the edge of the water (for the Jordan overflows all its banks all the days of harvest), that the waters which were flowing down from above stood and rose up in one heap, a great distance away.... So the people crossed opposite Jericho. And the priests who carried the ark of the covenant of the Lord stood firm on dry ground in the middle of the Jordan while all Israel crossed on dry ground, until all the nation had finished crossing the Jordan. (Jos 3:11, 14-17)

The Israelites had camped east of the Jordan looking west, perhaps several miles from the Jordan, and several miles more from Jericho. After forty years they had a second chance, one they had waited for a long time. That morning when the sun rose, it rose on a scurrying camp ready for the most important day of their lives. Probably the rams' horns had awakened them at dawn, and the cry went out all over that camp. This was no small camp; there were millions now. The priests of God and the Levites were carrying the cry across the camp: "Behold, the ark of the covenant of the Lord of all the earth is crossing over ahead of you into the Jordan!"

The people rose up, prepared themselves, and stood watching. Even those who couldn't see knew that somewhere in the heart of the camp the priests had taken down the tabernacle, and in proper manner had put the staves through the rings on the ark, covered the ark with all of its proper coverings, and were preparing to move toward the Jordan. They watched as the ark of the covenant, the testimony of his faithfulness to them, began to move out slowly. For a long time nobody moved.

For perhaps thirty minutes or more they watched this tiny box under its coverings until the box was barely visible and even the men themselves became remote in the distance.

Finally Joshua and the leaders began to move out, three-fifths of a mile behind the ark. The fathers turned to the mothers and the children and said, "It's time to go." The little ones couldn't see anything except the stirring of the adults, and some of the adults couldn't see anything except the motion in front of them. But in the order of the tribes and families, they deliberately moved toward a river that was raging, toward a land, toward giants, toward walled cities, toward war.

The Boundary Between Wandering and Purpose

But mainly they moved toward the boundary between wandering and purpose. They were coming out of wandering, finally, after forty years. They were coming out of gathering manna every day, and they were going into a land of their own to become farmers and craftsmen. They were on the verge of establishing a new culture. They were about to cross the point of no return.

God would get them in, but he would not get them out. He would open the waters for them to enter, but not for them to go back. Their backs would be to the river once they crossed, and they would have to fight their way into the land. They had committed themselves to the point of no return.

The priests made their way to the edge of the river, with the nation following behind them, and the waters were still moving. But they continued into the water because they bore the ark of God. Sometimes the waters don't stop for us until we've put our feet right in them. But nevertheless, when their covenant feet, bearing the ark of the covenant of God, touched the waters, creation stood in respect before the Presence of the living God.

The Presence that brooded over that ark was the same Presence that had brooded over the waters in Genesis 1 and called the dry ground to come forth. The waters don't respect leaders. But the waters respect the Presence that God's anointed leaders bear.

No Turning Back

Once on the other side, the leaders of the twelve tribes were instructed to return to the middle of the river bed, where the priests still stood with the ark of the covenant, and the leaders took stones with which they built a memorial to God (Jos 4).

I love the covenant Presence of God. It will stand and stay and not move until all the work has been done. The Presence of God stood in the Jordan that day until every last Israelite and every bit of their possessions had passed over to the other side. It stood while the leaders came back to get the stones for a memorial. Not until then did the Presence move.

If you follow the Presence, the Presence will lead you past the point of no return. It leads you to a place where you have no other alternatives. There's nothing else you think about doing, because your life has been poured into the purpose of God. That's when the victory will come and we will know the delivering power of God.

Whenever you pass the point of no return with God, he will be faithful to reveal himself to you in a new way. The Israelites had known him in many ways. They had known him as the Lamb, as the Healer, as the Baptizer, as the Deliverer, and as their Provider. But they were about to meet him in a brand new way—as Captain.

Faith always comes down to a point of action, a step we must take. Where is the Presence of God moving in your life?

At a time of dilemma in my life I asked a friend who was

older in the Lord and whom I respected, "How do you know what to do?"

He said, "I've always tried to follow where I thought the anointing was moving. I've always tried to do what I sensed God was doing, no matter how strange it seemed. And I've never been disappointed."

At that moment I took a big step. I gave up my salary, gave up things I had depended on, and took a new step. In the process I met God that day in a new way. It had nothing to do with salary or anything else. It was simply being willing to follow the Presence.

You may be facing a big decision. You may be wrestling with whether to change some of the things you're doing. Whatever the issue is, let me encourage you to follow the Presence. Make it your point of reference. If it leads you into deep waters, don't be afraid. The waters will stand still for the Presence. On the other side, when you've passed the point of no return, I believe with all my heart God will reveal himself to you in a new way.

I heard Ern Baxter say, "If Columbus had turned back, nobody would have blamed him. But nobody would have remembered him, either." Columbus fought all odds and even his crew to continue his voyage. You can turn back, but you'll miss the discovery that God has for you. Pressing on in the Presence is rewarded by a new revelation of God and a higher level of his provision.

NINE

Preparation for Victory

I TRUST THAT ONE RESULT OF READING this book will be that your sense of victory will be reinforced. I hope that you will not merely accommodate the world, or accommodate the enemy, but commit to do God's will, to fulfill the purposes and promises of God for his creation.

The Lord has a concern for creation; he made it; he loves it; through Jesus Christ he redeemed it. From the very beginning, man was placed here to rule over the work of God's hands. I believe that God is no less concerned about creation now than at the beginning. We are the sons and daughters of God to rule over creation, to be stewards of it, to bring righteousness, peace, and joy into it by the Holy Spirit, and to see it flourish and bring forth glory and honor to God.

There will be one day a new heaven and a new earth when old things will pass away, and I believe that the Lord's creation— all of it, what we see and what we don't see—will be perfectly and resplendently under his government. That will come in fullness when he appears to firstly put down all opposition and give us immortal bodies. For that day we all live, the day when the full manifestation of the government of the Kingdom of God on the earth shall be. Isn't that something to look forward to? But the Kingdom of God is also now. The Kingdom of God is in our midst. God's government is a reality now, as he reigns *in* us and *through* us.

The Objective of Combat

We are here to win. General George Patton said, "The only mission in combat is to win. If you do not win, you can forget everything else." It is important to remember that our task is the most serious of all struggles. All of the things we've talked about—commitment, information, obedience, following the Presence, remembering God—are related to the final issue of winning. None of them is an end within itself. Commitment is not an end in itself. Relating covenantally is not an end in itself. Relationship without purpose is not enough. The power of the Holy Spirit is not an end in itself. But all of these things are gifts and ways of God to bring us to the ultimate victory which is ours in Christ Jesus.

We need to become more win-oriented, more victory-oriented. Whether we live to see it all or not, we ought to die in the belief and the faith that Christ reigns, that one day his reign will be made visible, and everyone will bow and confess that Jesus Christ is Lord to the glory of God.

Spiritual Renewal

I'd like us to consider now the preparation for the victory that we see in Joshua 5:

Now it came about when all the kings of the Amorites who were beyond the Jordan to the west, and all the kings of the Canaanites who were by the sea, heard how the Lord had dried up the waters of the Jordan before the sons of Israel until they had crossed, that their hearts melted, and there was no spirit in them any longer, because of the sons of Israel. At that time the Lord said Joshua, "Make for yourself flint knives and circumcise again the sons of Israel the second time." So Joshua made himself flint knives and circumcised the sons of Israel at Gileath-harraloth.... For all the people who came out [of Egypt] were circumcised, but all the people who were born in the wilderness along the way as they came out of Egypt had not been circumcised. (Jos 5:1-5)

There were a number of things that God did to get them ready for victory. Some of us want to rush into the victory but are not prepared for it. But God will prepare us for what we have to face if we will let him.

Restoring the Covenant Tokens

We have already considered several aspects of preparation, such as commitment, spying, and following the Presence, but part of the preparation was the restoration of the covenant tokens. The Israelites had neglected the covenant, and the tokens of the covenant, while they were in the wilderness. Two things are specifically mentioned here that were vital tokens of the covenant that God gave to them.

Circumcision. When God made the promise to Abraham that he would give him a son and that in this seed all nations would be blessed, he gave him a sign: circumcision, the cutting away of the flesh. It was a very unique and unusual sign among all the nations. God gave it for a very special reason to indicate that he would bless Abraham's seed and that they would be abundant and bless all nations through the Branch—the Messiah—who would come forth from his descendants. It was a very vital sign; every son was commanded to be circumcised.

However, an entire generation had neglected it. The generation that came out of Egypt was circumcised, but they didn't pass along the covenant sign to their sons. So God said, "Before you go any further, I have a few things we have to get straight."

Notice that God had already brought them into the Promised Land. He had already done many things for them. The same is often true for us. The further we go with the Lord, the more he deals with us, the more we have to get straightened out. God will do a number of powerful things in your life, and sometimes you will say, "Well, praise God, now we're rolling easy."

But God will say, "Do you want to go any further?"

"Oh, I do."

"Well, there's something you and I have to get straight."

"I thought everything was straight."

"I just didn't want to bring it up yet. You weren't ready for it. But now I have to bring it up."

He keeps doing that. You may be facing something now that ten years ago wasn't important. Suddenly, it has become important. You keep saying, "But God, this thing really isn't 'bad.' I know a lot of people who do it." But God just keeps bringing it up.

Years ago it was tobacco for me. When God brought it to my attention, I had a lot of justifications. Charles Spurgeon, one of the great preachers, smoked. A lot of good people smoked. I was a Christian; I loved the Lord. But I just liked tobacco . . . no, I didn't like tobacco; I *loved* tobacco. I would have made tobacco sandwiches if I could have found a spread to go with it. I had a craving for it, and God kept confronting me with it.

What the Israelites faced was far more important than tobacco. We are talking here about covenant signs—circumcision—something as important as the observance of communion is to us.

You can't trifle with God. When Moses—that great man of God—was met by the Lord while tending sheep in the wilderness, the Lord said, "I want you to go deliver my people." So Moses started off, but the Bible says that God met him in the way and sought to kill him (Ex 4:24-27). Now, that's a strange thing. Can you put yourself in Moses' place? He had seen the fire, had gotten his mission settled with God (after an argument), and had started off to do what he was supposed to do. But on the way God met him and was ready to kill him if Moses kept going. What God said to Moses is a little like what Bill Cosby's dad said to him: "I made you, and I can make another one just like you." God said, "You are not going any further until we deal with this!"

Moses said, "Wait a minute, Lord. You're the one I just met up on the mountain. You are the one who told me to go."

God said, "I know it, but there's something you have to get straight."

"Why didn't we talk about it up there?"

"Well, you might not have gone if I had brought it up earlier, but I'm telling you now."

God doesn't trick us. But he doesn't always show us the future and things that we must face later. In this case, God wasn't springing something new on Moses. Moses knew that he had neglected to do something, something required by the very covenant he was fulfilling. So God said, "You have to circumcise your son."

God will let you come a long way and get you to a certain place, then say, "No. You can't go any further until you get something straight."

The question is: *Do you really want to win? Do you want to win badly enough to deal with the things God brings to your attention?* The issue is not whether you like what he is telling you. The issue is not whether you really want to do it. But the issue is: Do you want to win badly enough to do whatever you have to do to win?

The issue for me was not did I like tobacco. That really didn't matter. The issue wasn't even what other people thought about it. It was: Did I want to do God's will for my life and was I willing to remove an obstacle in my life? The issue wasn't even whether or not it was a sin. Sometimes we get all "hung up" in the moral ramifications of a thing and forget how it relates to the purposes of God. That's the issue—*getting rid of anything that hinders the will of God in our lives.*

The will of God is what we want to obtain. Some people would get rid of something in their lives if you told them it was a sin, but they don't care about aligning themselves with the will of God. We need to align ourselves with the will of God and get rid of everything that doesn't relate to the will of God, whether it looks like sin or not.

Sometimes we want to go as far as we can while staying legal. When we operate that way, we're not thinking about the will of God; we're just saying, "Legally, it's all right."

I had a friend several years ago who was a vegetarian because he belonged to a religion that required this. Personally, I love beef, but he was always bothering me about my eating it. One day I looked over at his plate, and he had something on it that looked just like meat. So I asked him, "What happened to you? Did you backslide? You have meat on your plate."

He said, "No, no, no. It's not meat. It's a meat substitute. It looks like meat, smells like meat, tastes like meat. But it's not meat."

I said, "It looks like sin, smells like sin, tastes like sin. But it's not sin?"

A lot of people are like that. They want something that's as close to sin as they can get without actually sinning.

I expect there were many family fights out there in the wilderness when God told the Israelites that they were going to be circumcised. With several million people discussing the whole thing, you can imagine some of the comments:

"We've gotten along this far without it."

"You mean, all the males, the boys too, even babies?"

"You mean we have to do . . . I thought that was outdated. What kind of a God do we have here?"

There's also a strategic aspect to this circumcision: one reason a Jewish soldier made such a fierce fighter was that he could never lie about being a Jew. The covenant sign was on him. His fight was unto death. You can't lie about being a covenant man.

Passover. Verse 9 describes what happened.

> Then the Lord said to Joshua, "Today I have rolled away the reproach of Egypt from you." So the name of the place is called Gilgal to this day. While the sons of Israel camped at Gilgal, they observed the Passover on the evening of the fourteenth day of the month on the desert plains of Jericho. (Jos 5:9, 10)

Only the circumcised could participate in the Passover; therefore, the Israelites had neglected the Passover also. The Passover was important because it was the remembrance of their salvation when they painted the blood on the doorposts before coming out of Egypt; it was a sign of God's covenant with them. He had said, "Every year, observe Passover!" It was to be a high and holy day, but they hadn't been observing Passover as God had commanded.

So he required that they remember where they came from, that they remember the covenant, and that they remember the blood and their salvation. They had to begin faithfully to observe those things which God had commanded them to observe.

Securing the Moral High Ground

The Bible says we have to be able to answer with a good conscience. The Scripture says that God is ready to punish all disobedience when our obedience is complete (2 Cor 10:6).

Think about that a minute; it is a very significant principle. Does it have relevance to something you are facing in your life today? We can't take shortcuts and be the people of God. We have to be clear in our conscience if we are going to fight the enemy. We have to know that we are standing right with God.

Sun Su, who wrote the ancient book on warfare, *The Art of War,* said, "If you want to win, you have to find the moral high ground." You have to know that you are standing in a righteous position before you go to war. War is won by those who believe in their cause. It may take them longer, but people who sincerely believe in their cause will die for what they believe.

If there is sin in your life, if the enemy has you under condemnation, if you're not sure where you stand, get that straight before you take on the enemy. Get it clear in your heart. Get on the moral high ground before God. God doesn't give ground to people based on their names, or on their skills. He gives ground based on whether they find favor with him in his righteousness.

God doesn't give us ground because we call ourselves Christians, God will give us ground when we stand righteously before him. If we live unrighteously, God will take the land away from us and give it to somebody who is righteous. Just because we are Americans or Canadians or some other nationality, we are not entitled to anything. We're only entitled to what God gives us, and he'll only give ground to us if we'll rule it the way he says to rule it. Any people who forsake the moral high ground forsake their best interest and their inheritance.

I believe that the Spirit of conviction precedes the Spirit of triumph. The Spirit of conviction is not here to hurt us. He is not here to rub our faces in our sin. He is here to get us on the moral high ground so we can walk with confidence before the throne of God and know that he will give us the battle.

Becoming Responsible

Before they were ready to take the land, these people had to be transformed from wanderers to Kingdom citizens. To do that, God gave them a new concept of his provision.

And on the day after the Passover, on that very day, they ate some of the produce of the land, unleavened cakes and parched grain. And the manna ceased on the day after they had eaten some of the produce of the land, so that the sons of Israel no longer had manna, but they ate some of the yield of the land of Canaan during that year. (Jos 5:11, 12)

Other than the samples brought back by the spies forty years earlier, this was the first time the Israelites benefited from the fruit of the land. It was something God did to prepare them for conquest.

Just because God delivers you out of bondage and sets you free, like he did the Israelites, you don't automatically understand everything you need to know. People have to train to become citizens of the Kingdom of God. God has to take the ways of the world out of us and train us to live under his government. We have to learn to work the land and make it productive through kingdom principles and stewardship.

Breaking the Cycle of Dependency

Giving Israel an inheritance was one thing; training them to take it and to rule it was quite another. Because of generations of slavery, their whole view of themselves and their responsibility had to be transformed. Here were some of the internal issues that they had to face:

1. They were dependent on the world's system. When these people were in Egypt, their concept of provision was dependence on the world's system. They were slaves. They had the mentality of slaves, in which their sense of identity, of self-worth, of confidence, was marred if not destroyed. Sometimes it takes generations to overcome being dependent, looking to someone else to provide for all needs.

Slavery is bad, but one thing it does is provide for you because whoever owns you will usually take care of you in order to maintain their "property" and keep you enslaved. Slavery is a terrible thing, but when you are set free from it, you are left—if you are not careful—with an attitude of dependency.

Many of us have been enslaved to the world and have become dependent on it. We talk about Jesus Christ taking over the world, but most of us wouldn't know what to do if the world's system collapsed because that's the only thing we have. If the economy fell apart or our job ended, we wouldn't know how to trust God.

2. *They were still dependent in the wilderness.* In the wilderness they learned to depend upon the Lord, and that's better because the source is sure. But theirs was not a condition of maturity. They were still an unproductive people. Their provision had to come down out of heaven. They had to have a miracle every morning for breakfast, and God obliged—for the time being.

They saw more miracles in the wilderness than the average Christian sees in a lifetime. These people in the wilderness weren't ignorant of the power of God. But they were ignorant of his will that they become mature and productive. They had learned to trust God for their provision, and that was good as far as it went, but they hadn't learned to be productive. They hadn't learned stewardship over anything, and if you'll remember the Garden of Eden, that's one of the tasks God has for his people.

Ultimately we are all dependent upon God, even for the very air we breathe. He is the Creator and sovereign over all. But it is also his good pleasure to invite us into the role of stewardship over his creation, to allow us to rule the land under his Lordship. He allows us to share in his rule because it's an exercise that develops us into the kind of people who can have a deeper, more mature relationship with him.

3. *Canaan is the place of Stewardship.* In Egypt, they were slaves and depended upon the world system for sustenance. They were God's people but slaves, nevertheless. In the wilderness, they were free but immature and unproductive. Each day like children they looked to God for supernatural provision. He gave it but longed to bring them into maturity, purpose, and productivity. In Canaan, it was time to grow and learn to work with God to make creation fruitful—to take the land. They not only conquered giants, they conquered the land

itself and governed it in such a way as to make it fruitful.

In Egypt, the system was the source. In the wilderness, heaven was the source. But in Canaan, the land was their source as long as they obeyed God. In Egypt they were poor. In the wilderness they had enough, but in Canaan they could have abundance.

In the wilderness, you aren't a steward over anything. But in Canaan, God gives you a patch of ground and says, "Drive the enemy off of it, cultivate it, and make it increase. And if you obey me, I'll make it rain when it's supposed to. But if you don't, it's going to get mighty dry." In the process you become mature and learn to work *with* God to bring abundance out of what God has given you.

Godly people have an innate desire to steward the land, to farm and tend it. They want to see God rain his blessing on the land and see fruit come up out of it. They want to see abundance. The Kingdom of God is abundant in righteousness, peace, and joy. It's productive.

Under the Canaanites, the land was dry and rocky. It was cursed. God couldn't bless their efforts. But to take the land and steward it, the Israelites would have to go through attitudinal changes about their dependency. Now they were committed to the land; they had been circumcised. They were observing Passover and ready to take responsibility for productivity. But just across the valley the giants were still there. The fort was still there, and God hadn't yet told them *how* they were to defeat the enemy.

TEN

The Conquest

THE ISRAELITES WERE PREPARED, but so far they didn't have any instructions about taking Jericho. Then Joshua received a *visitation*, and we read about it beginning in Joshua 5:13:

> Now it came about when Joshua was by Jericho, that he lifted up his eyes and looked, and behold, a man was standing opposite him with his sword drawn in his hand, and Joshua went to him and said to him, "Are you for us or for our adversaries?" And he said, "No, rather I indeed come now as captain of the host of the Lord." And Joshua fell on his face to the earth and bowed down, and said to him, "What has my lord to say to his servant?" And the captain of the Lord's host said to Joshua, "Remove your sandals from your feet, for the place where you are standing is holy." And Joshua did so. (Jos 5:13-15)

Visitations are for strategic reasons. God visits his people for a purpose. I believe that every time God has given a major visitation to Israel or the church it was because they needed to be prepared for something that was about to happen. God wanted his people to get ready for something, and so he needed to give them special instructions. When God visited Noah, there was a flood coming. When God visited Abraham, he wanted to separate him from the wicked system of Ur and the whole Babylonian system. When God visited Moses, he wanted to separate Israel out of Egypt. When God visited at Pentecost, it was to prepare the church for its separation and worldwide mission.

Meeting God in a New Way

Can you feel the heaviness that must have been on Joshua, the sense of need as he walked along? He had two or three million people camped there with all their belongings. The river was at their backs and Jericho was near.

Of course, it wasn't totally bleak. The enemy was afraid because they knew the river had opened up for these strange invaders. The Bible says that there was no more spirit in the people of Jericho. So it wasn't as though the Israelites didn't have something going for them. But they couldn't just stay by the Jordan and they couldn't go back; they had to go forward. The fort in front of them had double walls and locked gates.

So Joshua was walking along thinking about all this. He was thinking about all those powerful exortations that he had given and of how they had marched over the river. Now here they were in the land, and he didn't know what to do next. "What are we going to do next, God? I need help. What would Moses have done?"

The Scripture says that he was just walking along, and he looked up and saw a man with a drawn sword. Now, in that culture when a man had his sword drawn, that meant full alert was in order. People didn't draw the sword in vain. It was a tense situation, and Joshua had an automatic response. He challenged, "Are you for us or against us?"

I believe it was Jesus Christ whom he saw, a "Christophany" or supernatural manifestation of the Son of God "out of season," outside the thirty-three years we normally think of as his incarnation on earth. One of the reasons for believing this is that Scripture itself calls this messenger "the Lord" in the second verse of the next chapter (see Jos 6:2).

The Lord had condescended to appear to Joshua as a warrior. He did not appear as an unusual man, but a man with his *sword drawn*. Joshua looked up and saw him and said, "Are you for us or against us?" That's a very good question at a moment like that—it's logical. "Whose side are you on?"

Our Agenda Is Not the Issue

Notice the way the Lord responded to Joshua. He said, "Neither one. You have it all wrong. I'm not for you or against you. I'm the *Captain*. You are missing the point. I'm not here to help *you*. You are here helping me. I'm not on *your* side. I'm the Captain of the Lord's army."

Then Joshua fell down and said, "Do you want to say anything to me?"

And he answered, "Yes. Get your shoes off. You are on holy ground." God wanted to be sure that Joshua understood that he was dealing with the Sovereign God, not with someone who had merely come to give *him* assistance. Joshua had his perspective cleared up right there.

What I want you to see is: *we* are not the issue. When we are praying, "God, help us," we expect God to assist us because we think we are the issue. We tend to interpret everything according to how it relates to us. I evaluate this brother according to how he relates to me. I appreciate this sister according to how she relates to me. I judge this church according to how it relates to me. Will it help me? Will it help me do what I want? Is that movement *for* me? Is it *against* me? And I end up interpreting the whole world according to me.

But when Joshua came to the Lord asking, "Are you for me or against me?" the Lord answered, "You have it all wrong, Joshua. You are not the issue, I'm the issue. I'm the Captain. It's what I want to do that counts."

He met God in a new way. Israel was about to become an army.

God's Will Is the Issue

Don't ever think that you have met God in all the ways that he is going to reveal himself to you. When the Lord delivered the Israelites, they met him as the Lamb of God. When they went out into the waters, they met him as the Baptizer. When the cloud came on them, they met him as the Baptizer in the Holy Spirit. When they got out in the wilderness, they met him as the Provider. When they went a little further, they met him as the Healer. And when they crossed the river again, a new generation met him as the Baptizer. But this day they him met in a new way. They met him as the Captain of the Army. And before we can take the land, we have to know him as our Captain.

Perhaps you know Jesus as the Lamb of God and as your Baptizer, as your Healer and your Provider. If not, you should. But there is a land out there that God wants you to take; before it can be done, you must know him as the Captain of the Army, as a man of war. We will see him with his sword drawn. He is the Lord of God's army.

That's not very exciting to some of us because we are happy with the provisions; we are happy with the healings; we are happy because we're going to heaven. Those are all good things, but the issue is not us. A lot of us would be happy if we had a more significant ministry or enough money. But Jesus Christ won't be satisfied until the kingdoms of this world become the Kingdom of God to the glory of the Father.

The issue is the will of God. If we can contribute to that as a private in the army, then so be it. I want to see the Lord's people win. I want to see it more than *I* personally want to win. We must come to a place where we see the corporate success of the people of God above our own personal success.

Marching Orders

When God visited Joshua, he gave him instructions. God visits you for a reason. He knows where the key is. He knows where the enemy's achilles heel is. He knows where the devil is vulnerable. When God shows himself to us and speaks to us, we need to listen for his instructions. They might be strange instructions, but if you try to run your life by logic, you will miss the blessing because God's ways aren't our ways.

One old illiterate preacher was asked, "Do you use notes when you preach?"

He replied, "Son, the devil himself doesn't know what I'm going to say."

When we operate only by logic, I think the enemy reads our minds. Sometimes we announce to him so far in advance how we are going to do everything that he gets ready for us. Don't tell him everything you plan. Surprise him once in a while.

God's Will, God's Way

We need to know that we can't win without God's plan, which will differ in every location and for every person. That's why we must have more than principles; we must be sensitive to the Holy Spirit.

In 1967 I felt God spoke to me to invite Nicky Cruz to our city. He was mentioned in David Wilkerson's book, *The Cross and the Switchblade,* and when I met him in Miami, I asked him if he would come to Mobile, he said he would. I told him that we would have the city theater; I committed myself.

I went back home, and the city theater was available; everything seemed fine. So I started calling up all the people who I thought would be interested in helping us, but nobody was interested.

I was out on a limb.

I had acted unilaterally. I couldn't blame anybody. I had

thought it was the Holy Spirit telling me to invite Nicky. So I said, "What am I going to do?"

I was in my office praying, telling God about the situation and trying to let him know what was going on (as though he didn't already know), when God spoke to me and told me to call up a particular minister.

Now, it wasn't unusual for me to call on a fellow minister, but it was for me to call this particular minister. I guessed that he was so liberal that he was somewhere "to the left of the communist party" and I'm politically and theologically conservative. Well, I rebuked the idea for awhile to see if it would go away, but God said, "Do you want to have the meeting or not?" So, finally I got on the telephone.

When the minister answered, I must have sounded like I was going through a voice change, but I just spit it all out: "Hello-this-is-Charles-Simpson-and-I'm-pastor-of-Bayview-Heights-Baptist-Church-and-Nicky-Cruz-is-coming-to-Mobile-and-I-want-to-invite-him . . ." I just ran it all out at once.

He didn't know Nicky Cruz. He didn't know me. He didn't know anything, but when I got through, he said, "Yes that'll be fine. I'll tell you what. You can use my facilities, and I'll give you my staff, and I believe we can raise some money. It sounds like a great idea."

When I hung up, I thought, *He didn't say any of that. I know he didn't say any of that. How could that minister who is so wrong about so many things be so right about this? This man couldn't do that.*

Sometimes we have it all in our head how God is going to do something: God's going to use some good Bible-believing brother who believes the way we do—the right way, of course—and it's going to go just this way. But I'll tell you what happened in the Nicky Cruz meeting. That minister and his associate both had experiences with the Lord. The president of the ministerial association was filled with the Holy Spirit. The auditorium was full and running over; it was a tremendous meeting. But I truly believe that if I had not obeyed the Lord at that moment, it never would have happened.

The Plan

Let's read God's instructions to Joshua and Israel.

> Now Jericho was tightly shut because of the sons of Israel; no one went out and no one came in. And the Lord said to Joshua, "See, I have given Jericho into your hand, with its king and the valiant warriors. And you shall march around the city, all the men of war circling the city once. You shall do so for six days. Also seven priests shall carry seven trumpets of rams' horns before the ark; then on the seventh day you shall march around the city seven times, and the priests shall blow the trumpets. And it shall be that when they make a long blast with the ram's horn, and when you hear the sound of the trumpet, all the people shall shout with a great shout; and the wall of the city will fall down flat, and the people will go up every man straight ahead." (Jos 6:1-5)

What's really involved in this plan?

1. Know the conclusion. The first thing in God's instruction is: "Now, before I tell you anything, I want you to know that I've already given it to you." The best way to start is to know the end before you begin. Start as though it is all finished, because it is. If you want to reach any objective, you have to know from God that it is already yours, or you are just striving in vain. If you don't know that, don't do any of the rest of it.

2. Operate with discipline. Second, he said, "I want you to get the men of war out marching around the city." Marching, just marching, takes practice. First you need to get a drill sergeant to work with the new recruits—with their heads shaved, of course. This alone would eliminate most people. They don't want their hair cut off. But the army doesn't give a choice. The army strips you of all your assumed dignity. They shave off all your individualities and regiment you for awhile. It's, "Hup, two, three, four. Oh, come on, now. You're out of step," until you can march together with the other men rather than strolling along at your own swagger.

Just marching, just learning to walk together in unity to the beat of the same drum for the same cause, that's preparation. There is something about marching together that is psychologically important because it teaches you to work with those around you and be a unit. Some people never learn to march, but they want to lead. They can't walk *with* anybody, but they want to lead everything.

Back to Joshua:

> Then he said to the people, "Go forward, and march around the city, and let the armed men go on before the ark of the Lord." And it was so, that when Joshua had spoken to the people, the seven priests carrying the seven trumpets of rams' horns before the Lord went forward and blew the trumpets; and the ark of the covenant of the Lord followed them. And the armed men went before the priests who blew the trumpets, and the rear guard came after the ark, while they continued to blow the trumpets. But Joshua commanded the people, saying, "You shall not shout nor let your voice be heard, nor let a word proceed out of your mouth until the day I tell you, 'Shout!' Then you shall shout!" So he had the ark of the Lord taken around the city, circling it once; then they came into the camp and spent the night in the camp. (Jos 6:7-11)

3. Wait for the signal. Can you imagine how the previous generation would have responded to these instructions? You can see why God didn't let them in. Can you hear two of them talking after the meeting if Moses had said what Joshua said: "Do you buy that marching plan of his?"

"Not on your life. That's the craziest thing I've ever heard. Those Canaanites won't just drive us out of this land; they are going to laugh us out."

"What do you think about the being silent part?"

"Well, nobody has ever told me to shut up. I talk when I want to talk. And the shouting. That's the most ridiculous thing. If I feel like it, I'll shout any time I want to shout. I don't want anybody to tell me when to shout!"

"You're right. That's the most domineering leader I've ever heard of in my life. I'm with you. If I feel like shouting, I'm going to shout. I don't care what anybody says. Jericho or no Jericho, I'm just going to follow God as *I* hear him."

But these people were not there that day. They were dead in the wilderness. And Joshua didn't respond out of fear of what the people would think. He faithfully communicated God's instructions as he received them. And the people obeyed.

The Battle

I mentioned in the last chapter that we secure the moral high ground *before* a battle by purifying our conscience through repentance and obedience. But attaining the strategic advantage *during* the battle comes from the very same thing—continued obedience. How easy it would have been to waver at this point, to send out a team to try and tunnel under the wall or sneak over it at night. How easy it would have been for the Israelites to yell a few choice insults at the enemy leaning over the wall as they marched around . . . "just to demoralize the enemy, you know." But the instructions were to march and keep silent.

Now Joshua rose early in the morning, and the priests took up the ark of the Lord. And the seven priests carrying the seven trumpets of rams' horns before the ark of the Lord went on continually, and blew the trumpets; and the armed men went before them, and the rear guard came after the ark of the Lord, while they continued to blow the trumpets. Thus the second day they marched around the city once and returned to the camp; they did so for six days. (Jos 6:12-14)

The Walls Come Down

Then it came about on the seventh day that they rose early at the dawning of the day and marched around the city in the same manner seven times; only on that day they marched around the city seven times. And it came about at the seventh time, when the priests blew the trumpets, Joshua said to the people, "Shout! For the Lord has given you the city.... So the people shouted, and priests blew the trumpets; and it came about, when the people heard the sound of the trumpet, that the people shouted with a great shout and the wall fell down flat, so that the people went up into the city, every man straight ahead, and they took the city. (Jos 6:15, 16, 20)

Suddenly after six days of silence, two or three million people shouted . . . not to *get* the victory, but because *they already had it*! If you are shouting because you've got it, because it's already happened, that's another sound! It was a roar like the roar of the sea. It was the shout of triumph. All of a sudden, those old walls began to crack and crumble; the outside wall fell down, the inside wall fell down, and every one of the soldiers went straight into the city. That day they plundered the citadel of hell. They took the gates down; they took the walls down. The land was falling into their hands.

Keeping Faith

And Joshua said to the two men who had spied out the land, "Go into the harlot's house and bring the woman and all she has out of there, as you have sworn to her." So the young men who were spies went in and brought out Rahab and her father and her mother and her brothers and all she had; they also brought out all her relatives, and placed them outside the camp of Israel. And they burned the city with fire, and all that was in it. Only the silver and gold and articles of bronze and iron, they put into the treasury of the house of the Lord. However, Rahab the harlot and her father's household and all she had, Joshua spared; and she has lived in the midst of Israel to this day. . . . (Jos 6:22-25)

Rahab, with her family gathered around, was brought over to the Israelites, and she was grafted into the lineage of Jesus Christ because she was a covenant woman who feared the Lord.

Something Big Is Going to Happen

I love the worship and the praise that's developing in the house of God. You see, it's only when our hearts get in tune with the purpose of God and the truths we've been considering that we can take the land. God is tuning us up for something big, something bigger than is happening in any one church.

I keep asking God to put it all together for me, but every time I look, I just see more pieces. I keep thinking I'm going to see the whole picture, but all I see is more pieces of the puzzle. It is a bigger picture than I thought it was. God just keeps adding people to it. He's not going to let any one group bring it all together!

God is doing a miracle in our time. I believe he is going to bring people out of all nationalities and religious backgrounds and theological expressions, and he will tune their hearts by the Spirit. A sound will come out of the church that will cause walls to fall down.

That wall-shattering shout will come when the people of God

   . . . have the will to war,

   . . . develop the courage to fight,

   . . . are informed about the ways of God,

. . . spy out the weaknesses of the enemy,
. . . get committed to the purposes of God,
. . . begin to follow the Presence of God,
. . . meet Jesus as the Captain of the Lord's army,
. . . learn to march together in the will of God,
. . . are confident of victory.

Then there will erupt a sound from the church that will shatter hell's gates because the glory of the Lord will be spreading throughout the earth; the glory of the Lord will fill all the earth as the waters cover the sea, and nothing will stop it.

At what point in all of this does the second advent occur? Will the next appearance of the Captain mean that he personally leads the march?

I believe that final victory will coincide with his appearing. The ultimate kingdom manifestation awaits the events of 1 Corinthians 15, our change into immortality. Meanwhile, the Captain has come and left us with a mandate. "Proclaim the goodness of the kingdom to all nations. Baptize and disciple them in all the things that I taught. And I'll be with you to the end of the age." To that end may we be courageous.

Other Books of Interest
from Servant Publications

The Challenge to Care
A Fresh Look at How Pastors and
Lay Leaders Relate to the People of God
by Charles Simpson

A personal, practical approach to extending Christ's care
through pastoral leadership. *$5.95*

Cry Freedom
The Story of Lida Vashchenko and Her
Remarkable Escape from Soviet Russia
by Lida Vashchenko

One of the Siberian Seven shares the tragedy and the triumph
of life as a Christian in Soviet Russia. The powerful and
dramatic true story of a family's suffering and final escape.
$5.95

Knowing You Are Loved
What It Means to Know with Certainty
that God Loves You
by John Guest

A new book, from the author of *Only a Prayer Away*, to
deepen our knowledge of God's love for us. *$5.95*

Available at your Christian bookstore or from:
**Servant Publications • Dept. 209 • P.O. Box 7455
Ann Arbor, Michigan 48107**
Please include payment plus $.75 per book
for postage and handling.
*Send for our FREE catalog of Christian
books, music, and cassettes.*